FROZEN IN TIME

SCOTT PITONIAK

FROZEN IN TIME

THE HISTORY OF RIT HOCKEY

RIT Press
90 Lomb Memorial Drive
Rochester, New York 14623-5604
http://ritpress.rit.edu

Book and cover design by Marnie Soom
Printed in the U.S.A.

ISBN 978-1-939125-17-0 (softcover)
ISBN 978-1-939125-20-0 (hardcover)
ISBN 978-1-939125-18-7 (e-book)

Library of Congress Cataloging-in-Publication Data

Pitoniak, Scott.
Frozen in time : the history of RIT hockey / Scott Pitoniak.
pages cm
Includes index.
ISBN 978-1-939125-17-0 (Softcover : alk. paper) —
ISBN 978-1-939125-20-0 (Hardcover : alk. paper) —
ISBN 978-1-939125-18-7 (Ebook)
1. Rochester Institute of Technology—Hockey—History. I. Title.
GV847.75.R64P57 2015
796.9620974789—dc23
2015007506

To everyone who has been kind enough
to read my stuff through the years.

CONTENTS

ACKNOWLEDGMENTS

Books are collaborative efforts, and I was once again fortunate to have an excellent team to support me on this project. A doff of the cap to the following people and organizations:

RIT Press, specifically Molly Cort, Bruce Austin, Marnie Soom, David Pankow and Laura DiPonzio Heise for seeing this book to fruition;

Longtime RIT sports information director J. Roger Dykes, who is a walking encyclopedia of RIT sports history and a good friend;

Current sports information director Joe Venniro and his staff, including Stephen Jaynes, for doing a yeoman's job tracking down photos, articles and statistics, and setting up interviews;

Jody Sidlauskas and Becky Simmons from the RIT archives department, who provided extraordinary assistance in gathering information and photographs and in answering numerous questions;

Bob Finnerty and his staff at RIT's *University News* department for setting up interviews and providing reams of newspaper and magazine clips;

The RIT photographers whose masterful work has helped bring this history to life;

RIT Athletics Director Lou Spiotti, men's hockey coach Wayne Wilson, women's hockey coach Scott McDonald, and RIT President Bill Destler for their time and insights;

Chris Lerch and Steve Schultz, for sharing their stories and providing essential background information;

All the players, coaches, administrators and fans involved with RIT hockey whom I've interviewed through the years;

All the writers and broadcasters who have covered the team. Your accounts of the people, places and events that have made RIT hockey so special made my job so much easier. Special thanks to current and former sportswriters and broadcasters Gene Battaglia, George Beahon, Scott Biggar, Randy Bloechl, Greg Boeck, John DiTullio, Gene Duffey, Gary Fallesen, Mitch Lawrence, Chris Lerch, Jim Mandelaro, Sal Maiorana, Kevin Oklobzija, Leo Roth, Randy Schultz, Ed Trefzger and Rick Wheeler.

My bride, Beth; my children, Amy and Christopher; and my granddaughter, Camryn Marie, for your loving support.

14

INTRODUCTION

My first exposure to the Rochester Institute of Technology hockey program came in February 1985, not long after I had joined the sports staff of the *Democrat and Chronicle* newspaper. I was a feature writer, columnist and general assignment reporter at the time, and one of my jobs was to fill in on a number of beats, including local college sports. The Tigers' men's hockey squad was just two years removed from the school's first-ever national championship, and after covering just a few games I realized that RIT had the talent to make a run at another title.

And, sure enough, that's what happened, as the Tigers defeated Bemidji University, 5–1, on March 23, 1985, in Schenectady to win the NCAA Division III ice hockey championship. I have vivid memories of that season—not only of star players such as Chris Johnstone, Chet Hallice and Blaise MacDonald and their glib coach, Bruce Delventhal, but also of the passionate, vociferous RIT fans, who routinely stuffed the 2,100-spectator capacity Ritter Arena to the rafters.

I remember there being a lot of pressure on that team to replicate the March Madness of two years earlier, when fiery Coach Brian Mason and the superb goaltending of All-American Dave Burkholder guided the Tigers to the first national title won by any sports team in the school's then-154-year history.

When the final horn sounded in the '85 championship game at Achilles Rink on the Union College campus, every player on the RIT team skated toward one of the goals and formed a celebratory dog pile on the ice. It was a scene of unbridled joy. "I'm so excited," yelled MacDonald, a colorful character and All-American defenseman, "that I have goose bumps on my fingernails!" Reporters die for quotes like those. His pithy words found a prominent place in my story that led the next morning's sports section.

Afterward, Delventhal joked that I had been a good-luck charm for the program and said he was going to ask my sports editor to put me on the beat full-time. But a month after the season ended, I landed the coveted sports beat at the paper—the Buffalo Bills (although it wasn't quite as coveted back then because they had become the dregs of the National Football League in the dark ages just before their momentous

Opposite: Members of the RIT men's hockey team hold aloft the 1985 NCAA Division III hockey championship plaque.

Chris Johnstone leaps into the air after RIT takes the lead against Lowell (Massachusetts) in the 1983 NCAA Division II semifinals.

Super Bowl run). After becoming a full-time columnist and sports-enterprise reporter five years later, I tried to keep my hand in RIT hockey coverage, contributing columns and features when I could. Throughout the years, I remained impressed with the program's consistent excellence, both on the ice and in the classroom, and the fans' Pacific-Ocean-deep passion and zany antics.

Researching and writing this book during the past 18 months has given me an even greater appreciation for RIT hockey and what it means to the school's students and alumni. It's enabled me to relive that 1984–85 championship season, and delve deeply into the school's two other title teams—the men's in 1983 and the women's in 2012—as well as the most memorable team in school history: the 2009–10 men's squad that reached the NCAA Frozen Four, just five years after making the quantum leap from Division III to Division I. As far as national exposure and excitement, no season can match that one. That was the year the Tigers proved they could compete with the crème de la crème of college hockey despite the fact that they, unlike their competition, didn't award athletic scholarships.

By no means does this book profess to be the be-all and end-all of RIT hockey. The goal was to try to capture the people, places and moments that have made the sport such a vital part of campus life and pride for nearly six decades. We've traced the school's hockey roots back to the humble beginnings of the late 1950s, when some enterprising students with a passion for pucks got the program off the ground, against daunting odds and obstacles. Those RIT hockey pioneers were a motley crew, to be sure, playing with hand-me-down equipment and tattered uniforms from the Rochester Americans minor-league hockey team. Initially, the Tiger skaters had no arena to call home. Financial support from the university was nonexistent. The

Ben Lynch (center) and Andrew Favot (left) celebrate a goal against Air Force during a Feb. 5, 2011 game.

players dug into their own pockets to rent time on an outdoor rink in the wee hours of frigid mornings because that was only time the sheet of ice was available. They played all of their games on the road, sardining themselves and their equipment into their own jalopies and plowing through snow and ice in the dead of winter in order to make their appointed rounds in places like Canton and Ithaca. Eventually, their persistence paid off. RIT students fell in love with the sport, and the growing interest was enough to prompt school administrators to acknowledge the team's existence as a legitimate club sport before adding it to the Tigers' intercollegiate athletic lineup in 1964. We also explore, in great detail, the challenges overcome by pioneering women like Sheila Stevenson in order to launch their program in the mid-1970s. She and the other founding mothers provide a profile in perseverance.

Support from students and alumni, particularly on game days, has been a driving force behind RIT hockey's extraordinary run. Over time, the Corner Crew, first in Ritter Arena and now in the Gene Polisseni Center, established itself as one of the most avid and loyal student cheering sections in college sports, with creative, at times profane, chants and a cast of characters who have become as much a part of program lore as the players and coaches themselves.

Hockey has clearly become a galvanizing force and a source of pride among the university's students, faculty and alumni worldwide. It's my hope that the stories told in the ensuing pages will give you a feel for this love affair between a school and a sports program.

Enjoy.

Scott Pitoniak

May 2015

RIT

1.

THE PUCK STARTS HERE

Jack Trickey vividly remembers being glued to the family radio as a boy growing up in Rochester, New York in the early 1950s, listening to National Hockey League broadcasts from Canada. He was enthralled by the word pictures painted by the announcers. Decades later he could still hear the sounds of steel skate blades carving up the ice, bodies being slammed into the boards encompassing the rinks and the thunderous roar of the crowd when goals were scored. "Even on the radio, you could feel the excitement and the speed of the game," he said in a 2013 interview.

Before long, Trickey and his neighborhood friends were purchasing skates and hockey sticks and heading off to a frozen pond at Ellison Park in suburban Rochester. They would shovel the snow off the pond to form their own primitive rink and skate for hours, pretending they were playing for the Montreal Canadiens or the Toronto Maple Leafs.

"You didn't have the organized youth leagues like you do today, and there wasn't any high school hockey," said Bill Whiteneck, a lifelong friend of Trickey's. "So, we'd play a lot of pickup games. Word spread about our games at Ellison and more and more kids showed up to see what it was all about. It was an awful lot of fun."

When Trickey first set foot on the Rochester Institute of Technology campus in downtown Rochester as a freshman student in the fall of 1957, he was disappointed to discover that the school didn't have even an intramural hockey team, let alone an intercollegiate program. A young man of action, Trickey was determined to do something about that. He circulated flyers around campus to gauge interest in forming a team. After receiving about a dozen responses from students who wanted to play hockey, Trickey decided to contact Ed House and Al Deeth, two former players with the Rochester Packers, a prominent amateur hockey team that played in 1954–55 and 1955–56 before disbanding. House and Deeth said they'd be happy to help Trickey form a league of several teams in the Rochester area.

"See, it wasn't just enough for me to field a team from RIT," Trickey said. "We needed to have teams for us to play. Ed and Al helped me make inquiries beyond the RIT campus and we discovered there were about 250 young men in the Rochester community that wanted to

Opposite: Early RIT hockey teams wore hand-me-down jerseys from the Rochester Americans minor-league team.

play hockey. So, we had enough people to form a league."

The next step was finding a place to play. House and Deeth arranged a meeting with Harold Rand, the director of the Rochester War Memorial, and they were able to work out a deal in which the newly formed Monroe County Amateur Hockey Association could use the rink on Monday nights. To meet the rental fee, which Rand lowered so that it would cover ice rental expenses and a nurse's fee, each player was required to pay 50 cents a week.

Trickey's hard work paid off as six teams (four at the senior, or 18-and-above, level and two at the junior level) began play in 1957. Four of the teams secured sponsors. The clubs that didn't find funding used makeshift equipment, such as old magazines for padding and regular winter gloves instead of hockey gloves. Most players couldn't afford uniforms, so Trickey came up with the idea that each team would choose a specific color and ask its players to buy same-colored sweatshirts.

"That way we'd at least have one team all in blue and another team all in red, so there was a little uniformity. It was pretty primitive, but we didn't care. The important thing was that hockey was being played."

While all this was going on, Trickey met with Lou Alexander, Jr., RIT's director of athletics, to inquire about hockey becoming a club sport. Club sports teams differed from intercollegiate teams in that they did not receive any financial backing from the athletics department. They could, however, receive aid from the school's student council. Alexander thought that would be a wise path to pursue, and in 1958 the RIT Hockey Club was officially formed.

Although Trickey's 1957 team was made up primarily of RIT students, it also featured some players who had no

RIT Hockey Club jacket, early 1960s.

affiliation with the school. In order for a club team to be officially recognized by the university, it would have to be composed solely of RIT students. That meant Trickey had to intensify his recruitment of students for the second season. During orientation week in the summer of 1958, he posted flyers about the hockey club in the dormitories and academic buildings throughout campus. He also manned a sign-up table in the lobby of one of the buildings that served as a quasi student center.

One of the students who stopped by that table was an incoming freshman from Buffalo named Allan Shepard. A veteran of numerous backyard and municipal hockey league games, Shepard was thrilled to learn that there was an opportunity to continue playing, and immediately signed up. "That was a real turning point for us because Al was a talented, intelligent player who was very passionate about the sport," Trickey said. "He was like a player-coach for us and was instrumental in really getting the program launched."

The word "launch" was quite appropriate because this was around the time when the NASA space program was beginning to take off, and one of its star astronauts happened to be a man named Alan Shepard, who became the first American to travel in outer space. RIT's Shepard, who was not related to the astronaut, joked about it.

"There were some guys on the team who later would call me "Spaceman," and I had people who wanted my autograph when they heard my name. Even when I told them I wasn't *the* Alan Shepard, they wanted me to sign things so they could pull a gag on friends. I didn't mind it. It was all in fun."

Allan Shepard

Shepard, who was inducted into the RIT Sports Hall of Fame in 2003, has been called "the father of the program." He's proud of that designation, but believes the program really had several "fathers" who helped it take flight. That is true, but Shepard proved to be the driving force. During his four years at RIT, hockey became the most popular sport on campus and the foundation was laid for the club team to become a varsity sport.

As was the case with the fledgling U.S. space program, the launch of the RIT hockey program endured its share of misfires. In 1958 the Tiger skaters were officially recognized as a club team, and the following season they received funding for the first time from the university's student council, which allocated a budget of $1,020 to purchase equipment to outfit 16 players. Although it was a start, that budget wasn't nearly large enough to cover expenses, which, in addition to equipment, included everything from ice rental time to referees' fees to uniforms.

The club caught a break when Rochester's minor-league hockey team, the Americans, decided to redesign their uniforms. The Amerks, as they were called, offered to sell their old jerseys to the RIT hockey club for a nominal fee. "It wound up working out perfectly," Shepard said. "These were beautiful, almost new wool jerseys—probably cost about $80 apiece back then—and they gave them to us for almost nothing. It was our good fortune that they had lettering that read "AMERICANS" across the chest. It just so happened that the "R" and the "I" were together. So, we went out and bought the matching "Ts" then took the jerseys over to the women's dorm (Kate Gleason Hall) and asked the girls if they could remove all the letters except the "R" and the "I" and sew on the "Ts." It was like it was meant to be."

To maximize their budget, the Tigers purchased

The 1960-61 men's club team had to play all but one game on the road.

items in bulk at a CCM sporting goods store in Buffalo and at another huge hockey equipment store just across the Canadian border in Guelph, Ontario. The trip to Canada required some shifty moves by the RIT hockey players. Marv Pozefsky, who played goalie and spent two years as club president, recalled one incident.

> When we arrived at the border, the officer asked us our reason for visiting and we told them we were an American college hockey team from Rochester going to Guelph to play a Canadian team. They saw that we had huge equipment bags in the trunk, so they let us go through. Well, what they didn't know is those bags were empty. We'd go to the sporting goods store in Guelph and buy as many sticks and pads and pucks as we could afford and stuff them into the bags. This was back when the Canadian dollar was worth 75 cents American, so we really made out with the exchange rate. On our way back, we were sweating bullets because if they opened up those equipment bags, they would see that we had a bunch of stuff that was brand new and we'd have to claim and pay additional fees. When we stopped at the border, the customs officers asked us the purpose of our trip. We told them we just got our asses kicked by some really good Canadian hockey teams and they just laughed and waved us through.

The Monroe County Amateur Hockey Association folded at the end of the 1959–60 season, but that was okay because the RIT hockey club had established itself to the point where it was ready to play in a collegiate league. In 1960–61, the club joined the Finger Lakes Hockey League and scheduled games against club teams from the University of Rochester, Ithaca College and the University of Toronto, as well as freshmen or junior varsity teams from Colgate, Cornell and Hamilton College. With the exception of the University of Rochester game, which was played at the Genesee Valley Park outdoor rink, all of RIT's games were on the road.

Because the team wasn't sanctioned by the athletics department, the players had to provide their own transportation to and from games. Instead of buses, they crammed into the four or five cars owned by players. According to Shepard, it took some creative maneuvering.

> Between those huge equipment bags and the players, we would be packed in there like sardines. Fortunately the cars were a lot bigger back then. We'd all chip in for gas. It was only about 40 cents a gallon back then, which was a good thing because if it was what it costs today, there wouldn't have been an RIT hockey program; we would have gone broke.

The Tigers also were on their own as far as lodgings. On one trip to the University of Miami in Oxford, Ohio, they slept on the living room and dining room floors at one of the player's houses before returning to Rochester. "We were actually late getting to that game because Bill McLean blew a transmission on his old Volvo," Shepard said. "Things like that happened."

On another trip, Shepard recalls being pulled over for speeding by the police in a small town. The officer took

Hockey skates worn by Tim Butler, 1960–1964.

the young men to the town justice's house, miles from the main road.

> He told us our fine was $100. We almost fainted because we didn't have that kind of money. He said, "All right, boys, I'll take whatever you have." So we scraped together all of our dollar bills and pocket change and gave it to him and he let us go. He cleaned us out of every cent.

Another time, the Tigers' five-to-six car caravan barreled through a blizzard to get to Ithaca, only to discover upon their arrival that the game had been canceled.

Shepard served as a player-coach during those early seasons. He would organize practices and put the team through drills. He'd also make up the lineup on game

HOCKEY CLUB
Kneeling: Fred Pickett, Wayne Jackson, Norm MacEachern, George Kanda, Tom Frahm, Chris Elias, Don Simonini, Kent Phibbs, Larry Laske, Chester Doverspike. *Standing:* Jack Blair, *Manager;* Jim Heffer, *Coach;* Dave Gallahue, Bill Geiger, Tim Butler, Douglas Michalske, Joe Rickard, Chris Hoagland, Douglas French, Ian Duff, John Polger.

Hockey Club photo from the 1963 *Techmila* (RIT yearbook).

nights. "Somebody needed to do it," he said, "because there wasn't any money allocated for a coach's salary." In 1961, Jack Dykema, the president of the Rochester-based Quality Containers Association, showed up at one of RIT's games at the War Memorial and offered to coach the team. Years earlier, Dykema had been a player of note at the University of Pittsburgh. Pozefsky remembered the team's reaction to its new coach.

> He knew his stuff and had a big-time hockey background, so we happily welcomed him aboard. We were upfront and told him we couldn't pay him and he was fine with that. I think he was bored and was looking for something hockey-related to do. Al had done a great job, but it's tough when you are a player and a coach and a student. Having a guy like Jack who could focus solely on coaching was another step in the evolution of the program.

Record-keeping from the first few years is sketchy, though Shepard and Pozefsky said RIT more than held its own against Monroe County Amateur Hockey Association competition. During the 1960–61 campaign, the club gained additional exposure when it played a game against the Rochester Rockets, a top-notch local amateur team, as part of a hockey doubleheader at the War Memorial in which the Amerks played the nightcap. RIT wound up splitting two games that season with the Rockets. The Tigers also defeated Ithaca College's club team and lost games to the Hamilton College and Colgate University freshmen.

One of the major challenges in the early years was finding ice time for practice.

"We were able to rent the outdoor rink at Genesee Valley Park, but our time slot usually was midnight to 1 in the morning, and it was quite a hike to get there," Pozefsky recalled. "There were some bitter, cold nights on that rink when I thought for sure we were going to suffer frostbite."

Unlike most of his teammates, Pozefsky didn't have any prior hockey experience. He had been a speed-skater growing up in Gloversville, New York, and showed up at the RIT hockey club's organizational meeting because he was bored and looking for a school activity in which he could become involved. "They asked me if I could skate and I said, 'Yes,' and they said, 'Well, why don't you see if you can play goalie?' and I did," Pozefsky said. "I obviously didn't realize what I was getting myself into, but I found out in a hurry." Before he faced his first shot on ice, he faced hundreds of shots in the RIT fencing room.

> Guys would come in and fire rolls of tape at me to simulate pucks. That's where I learned to make kick saves and fine-tune my reflexes. The great thing about the fencing room is that there were mirrors on the wall so I could study my form.

His first on-ice appearance in goal came in the first game of the season at the War Memorial. He chuckled as he described the situation.

> Let me tell you, making saves against hard rubber pucks on the ice in a game is a lot more difficult than making saves against rolls of tape in sneakers in a fencing room. Somehow, I managed to get through that first game and we won. But I don't think I've ever been so dead tired as I was after that game. I was a nervous wreck. I was completely drained.

FROM TECHMEN TO TIGERS

From the school's founding in 1829 until roughly 1955, RIT's athletic teams went by a variety of names, including the Techmen and the Blue and Gray, after the school's original colors. But according to an article in the October 11, 1963 issue of *The Reporter*, a new nickname began to take hold in the mid-1950s, thanks to the school's first undefeated basketball team and the enterprising leader of the RIT News Bureau. Harry Watts was so enthralled by the unbeaten 1954–55 hoopsters that he decided the team needed a name that expressed its "ferocious" style of play. After meeting with a group of RIT lettermen, it was agreed that future news releases would carry "Tigers" as the official nickname of all the school's sports teams. And that's what RIT's sports teams have been known as ever since.

The hockey club didn't have to travel far to find a solution for its ice-time problem. The answer was right there on campus. The Ritter-Clark Arena (now the Skating Institute of Rochester or SIR) had been built in 1955 with money from F. Ritter Shumway, who would become one of the most generous and influential benefactors in school history. Shumway was a figure-skating enthusiast who built the 600-seat arena with his favorite sport in mind. However, the rink also was constructed to hockey specifications, and after the RIT club team started to build a following on campus, the players looked at Ritter-Clark as a potential home. Pozefsky remembers the challenges.

> There were a couple of issues that we needed to overcome. Because the Genesee Valley Figure Skating Club practiced there, Shumway had installed thousands of dollars' worth of mirrors on the walls above the boards that encased the rink, so that skaters could study their form. That was going to be a huge problem for us because errant pucks obviously would turn those mirrors into thousands of pieces of shattered glass. Plus, there was concern that pucks would make black smudge marks all along those boards, which were pristine white.

After what Shepard termed "tortuous negotiations," he was able to convince rink manager Lewis Elkin to let him and his teammates practice there a few times a week at 11 p.m. Elkin had just one stipulation, and it was a big one: they couldn't use pucks. "That was the big joke," Shepard said. "Here we have this great hockey program in its formative stages and we can't use the piece of equipment that's essential to our game." In the beginning, Shepard and his teammates complied with the restriction.

> We formed some lines and skated some formations and kind of pretended we had this invisible puck. But that got old in a hurry. Imagine playing baseball or football or basketball or golf with all your equipment and no ball. We had to find some ingenious ways to get around that puck ban.

The first idea was to use balled-up black electricians tape as pucks. That worked until they started making smudge marks on the boards.

"We realized that if we kept doing that, Elkin would throw us out of the place," Shepard recalled. "So, we decided to wrap some white medical tape around the friction tape, and that wound up working. It still wasn't the same as practicing with pucks, but it allowed us to work with something that at least simulated hockey."

After being elected to the student council, Pozefsky worked on finding a better solution. He petitioned the council to allocate several thousand dollars to put up temporary boards over the mirrors to protect them from flying pucks. The council approved, and the hockey club found its first home. The change was a good one, according to Pozefsky.

> We no longer felt like nomads. It not only allowed us to practice like a real hockey team, but it also gave us an arena where we could play home games right on campus. We might have only been taking baby steps, but the important thing is that we were moving forward.

The other thing that continued to grow was the talent level of the RIT players. Tim Butler, a 1964 RIT graduate who spent two seasons as a team captain, recounted the program's evolution.

A hockey jersey worn by Allan Shepard, regarded by many as the father of the RIT hockey program.

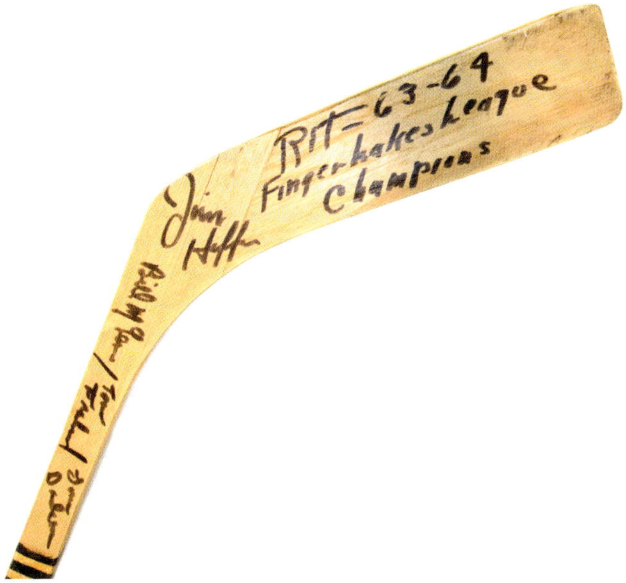

Hockey stick signed by members of the 1963-64 men's team, which went 17-0-1 – the only undefeated season in RIT hockey history.

To be honest, we were pretty lame at first—and I include myself in that category. We weren't seasoned players. But Al was very talented and I think he helped get the word out, and soon we were attracting some really good players. Bill McLean had played youth hockey in Montreal. Tom Frahm had been a goalie in the Chicago Black Hawks development program, so he wound up being a huge upgrade. We started getting guys from northern New York State and the Midwest, and guys like Norm MacEachern from Toronto. He still holds the school record for most goals in a game. He had a shot that was like a cannon. So, the quality of play was night and day from our humble beginnings.

Passionate student support also played a crucial role in the development of the program. Hockey became a galvanizing force on campus.

"When I first started attending RIT, the students were pretty apathetic," explained Shepard. "There wasn't much school spirit. There didn't seem to be anything to rally around. But I saw that change dramatically during my time there, and I think hockey definitely was a catalyst for change."

The Greek community was especially strong on campus in the late 1950–early 1960s. Shepard and several of his teammates were fraternity brothers, and they were able to drum up interest in their houses and convince their brothers and sorority sisters to attend hockey games. "I think half the guys on the team were in fraternities, and they helped sell the sport on

F. RITTER SHUMWAY

Although his passion was figure skating, F. Ritter Shumway wound up playing a profound role in the evolution of RIT's hockey program. A pond skater as a boy, Ritter fell in love with skating after seeing the Ice Follies in 1939. Following World War II, the graduate of Princeton and Oxford Universities began serious training in ice dancing and wound up winning numerous regional and national titles. Early in his training, Ritter discovered there was a dearth of places to skate in the Rochester area.

When RIT approached him about contributing to the construction of an athletic facility on its downtown campus, he said he would be happy to give, but he might be persuaded to dig a little deeper if the facility included an ice rink. That led to the building of the Ritter-Clark Arena, named partly in memory of Shumway's grandfather, Frank Ritter, an industrialist who, in 1885, helped found the Mechanics Institute, the forerunner to RIT. (The arena also was named in memory of benefactor George H. Clark, a former director of the Eastman Kodak Company.) Though constructed for figure skating, the rink also was regulation hockey size, and even included metal piping at opposite ends of the ice to accommodate the placement of hockey goals.

It took some shrewd negotiating on the part of the founders of the RIT hockey program in the late 1950s to convince the Ritter-Clark Arena manager to allow the players to use the facility, first for practice and later for games. With a seating capacity of 600, it, along with the War Memorial, was the program's original home rink.

F. Ritter Shumway and his skating partner, Harlene Lee

Before moving the program to its suburban Rochester location in 1968, RIT officials again asked Shumway if he would help fund the construction of a new arena on its Henrietta campus. He happily agreed, and the Frank Ritter Memorial Arena opened its doors in 1968—this time as a multipurpose building that would serve as a home to figure skating and hockey. It became an annual tradition for Shumway and his partner, Harlene Lee, to perform between periods of a home hockey game. Shumway was feted at the arena bearing his grandfather's name in 1987 on his 80th birthday. Among his gifts was an RIT hockey jersey with his name sewn onto the back.

Shumway died on March 9, 1992, just 18 days shy of his 86th birthday.

campus," Butler said,"Fraternities and sororities were a lot rowdier in those days and I think they fell in love with hockey because they discovered that it was a rough-and-tumble and noisy sport. You could really blow off a lot of steam at games. There's no question that the Greeks played a pivotal role in helping the sport take off at RIT."

Perhaps no one played a bigger role in fanning the flames of student interest than John Absalom.

"He's the unsung hero in our story,'' Shepard said. "He absolutely loved the sport, and he was constantly advocating on our behalf. And the funny thing is that here was a guy who didn't see his first hockey game until he showed up at RIT."

Indeed, the long-time Virginia resident admits he initially didn't know if a puck was made of vulcanized rubber or filled with air. But Absalom proved to be a quick study. "It was love at first sight," he said. And before long, the young man who played three years of varsity basketball at RIT and spent two years as sports editor of the student newspaper (*The Reporter*) became the program's most ardent and vocal supporter. In word and print, Absalom implored his fellow students to check out an RIT hockey game. He guaranteed they would fall in love with the sport, just as he had, and they also would discover what school spirit was all about. "I think he kind of gets overlooked," Shepard said. "But he was as much of a driving force as anybody in making hockey *the* sport at RIT."

Absalom used his forum as sports editor not only to encourage students to get behind the program, but also to badger the school's administration into allowing the hockey team to practice and play games at Ritter-Clark.

> You had this beautiful sheet of ice on campus, so why not make a few renovations so it can be used by the hockey team? To me it was a no-brainer. And it also was a no-brainer that the club team should become a recognized intercollegiate team, given the student support.

Like Shepard, Absalom decried student apathy and wanted to do something to stoke school spirit. He believed hockey could provide the spark. Of the nearly 2,000 games played in the program's 58-year history, few were more significant than the one against the University of Rochester at the War Memorial Auditorium on Saturday, November 11, 1961. It proved to be a watershed moment.

Absalom organized a pep rally on the campus quad prior to that night's game. During the festivities, he grabbed a megaphone and proceeded to the second floor balcony of Kate Gleason Hall, the women's dormitory known as the Kag. From that perch, he made an impassioned speech about the importance of school spirit as nearly 1,000 students shouted their approval and joined him in a series of cheers.

"It was an absolutely crazy scene, like some big revival meeting,"Absolom said. "Nearly the entire student population showed up. You would have thought we were giving away money."

And the scene only grew crazier after Absalom descended from the balcony and led the throng on a parade from campus through the streets of downtown to the War Memorial, which was only about four blocks away. "I felt like the Pied Piper," he said.

Several estimates said the RIT supporters outnumbered the UR crowd by nearly three to one."It was the largest crowd ever to witness an RIT sporting event, Shepard said. "There was this huge roar when we took the ice, and you could feel the adrenaline rush through you as you looked up into the stands and saw all those people from RIT there. I couldn't help but think back to how far we had come from those early games when the only people in the stands were our girlfriends."

It didn't take long for the rowdy RIT crowd to become even rowdier. Just six seconds after the opening faceoff, Shepard scored a goal. Nearly six decades later, he still gets goose bumps talking about it.

> Each of us experiences in our lives those special moments, when the stars and planets align perfectly. Well, that was one of those moments for me. I couldn't have scripted it any better.

Defenseman Bill McLean stole the puck and scored eight minutes and 36 seconds later to make it 2–0, and his brother, Jim, capped the scoring with a goal with just 17 seconds remaining in the game as RIT won, 3–0. The Tigers were so dominant that their goalie, Tom Frahm, needed to make only three saves.

"That game enabled us to claim local bragging rights, and that was important to me and my classmates," Shepard recalled. " See, UR was considered the white-collar university and we were considered the blue-collar university. We were perceived as the poor stepchild by many people in town; we were inferior. So, I guess we might have played with a little bit of a chip on our shoulders that night. That game really was a turning point for the program because it really endeared us to our student body and made them feel good about their school."

In the next issue of *The Reporter,* RIT's bimonthly student newspaper, there appeared an effusive editorial headlined: "Tigers Shatter 'Apathy Barrier.'"

> A myth was shattered Saturday evening, the myth that there is no spirit at all among the student body here, when well over 800 loyal sons and daughters of RIT descended upon the War Memorial to cheer their hockey Tigers to a shutout victory over the U of R varsity.
>
> They rallied at the quad, and then, led by Tiger Jack Absalom, marched to the scene of battle. There has been nothing like it since the D-Day invasion of Normandy.
>
> Whenever there was a Tiger goal, there was also bedlam-rattling garbage cans, confetti, a trombone and the peculiar eruption of the human vocal cords that is unmatched in any other species, and that has been immortalized by every Sunday crowd that ever saw a Dodger-Giant game at Ebbets Field.
>
> A lot of the credit for this must surely go to the pert and enthusiastic cheerleaders.
>
> The Tiger skaters demonstrated that the Institute has a team it can be proud of. They played with a dash and a confidence that was undoubtedly bolstered by the explosive cheering section above them.
>
> George Kanda, Tim Butler, Al Shepard, the McLeans and the rest looked like pros. The entire team had what it took to win. We can show our support and our faith in them by coming out en masse for the remaining games on the schedule. The team won't die if spirit's high.

Next to the editorial were several heartfelt letters about that seminal RIT hockey extravaganza. One was written by Bill Turri, a printing major.

> I have been a student at RIT for five years and Saturday, November 11, I realized what true college spirit is. Every one of these students was bursting with enthusiasm and pride for RIT. Those of you who are upperclassmen and weren't there probably think that I have RIT mixed up with a real college. But I haven't. It was RIT, RIT students, RIT spirit, RIT enthusiasm and RIT pride.

Turri went on to write about a school administrator who was not thrilled with Absalom and the raucous rally. His words dripped with sarcasm.

> She later got this gentleman (Absalom) aside and threatened him with social probation. He was guilty of stirring up pride for RIT and not running the rally correctly. How would anyone at RIT know how to run a rally? We have never had one before. That's right freshmen; that was the first rally in RIT history. I say it is about time that attention was drawn to RIT and all of its buildings, faculty and students. If we are allowed to have further rallies, we might even learn and sing RIT's alma mater.

Another student, Chuck Spring, a photo major, agreed with Turri's assessment that it was the greatest show of school spirit he had witnessed. He wrote: "Maybe this will kill the apathy talk, and maybe the apathy itself. We did it once, now let's keep it up."

Bob Burchard shoots on net during practice in the early 1960s.

As Shepard and his teammates had hoped, the RIT administration took note of the tremendous support shown by students and faculty. "I think it sent a message to the powers that be that hockey had become the BMOC—the Big Man On Campus—and that we deserved to take the next step and become an intercollegiate sport," Shepard said. "After that turnout, we felt like we no longer could be denied."

Not long after that game, RIT Athletics Director Lou Alexander Jr. asked Keith Mosley, the chair of the school's athletic committee, to investigate what it would take to add hockey to the university's sports lineup. As part of its study, the committee surveyed other colleges in the state and Northeast with hockey programs. Mosley wanted to determine the costs of running a program and also gauge the willingness of other schools to play varsity games against RIT should the Tigers go that route.

Momentum clearly was in the hockey club's favor. A few weeks before the seminal game with UR, the RIT student council polled 1,860 RIT students. Of the 1,042 respondents, 95 percent were in favor of seeing the Tigers hockey program enter intercollegiate competition. Nearly 92 percent said they would attend intercollegiate games at Ritter-Clark. Eighty-nine percent said they would attend an exhibition game at the War Memorial against an intercollegiate team.

On February 2, 1962, the Institute's athletic committee voted in favor of converting the hockey club to an intercollegiate team within the next three years. Mosley's group also recommended:

- refurbishing the Ritter-Clark Ice Arena in such a manner as to provide for practice and competitive facilities;
- scheduling 90-minute practice sessions between the hours of 5 p.m. and 8 p.m. three nights a week and setting aside six nights for home games to be played;
- requesting that the athletics director schedule a minimum of 12 games with hockey clubs, freshman teams and amateur teams for the next season;
- budgeting $6,000 (six times as much as had been budgeted for the current season) for the next season;
- authorizing employment of a part-time hockey coach; and
- increasing the student athletic fee from $12 to $15 a year, effective 1963–64, to help fund the hockey program as well as the rink's renovations.

In making their recommendations, the committee cited the work done by members of the hockey club to get the program off the ground and the ardent student support. Thirteen days later, the student council seconded the committee's recommendation that hockey become an intercollegiate sport and urged that the athletics department take over management and promotion of the team. The proposal was then passed on to school President Dr. Mark Ellingson and the board of trustees. They, too, believed the timing was right, and the wheels were set in motion for hockey to become the school's ninth intercollegiate sport.

Although Shepard and the other upperclassmen would be alumni by the time the RIT hockey team played its first intercollegiate game, they couldn't have been happier with the news.

"Yes, we would have loved to have taken part in that first game," Shephard said. "But we took solace in knowing that our sacrifices, as well as the sacrifices of people like Jack Trickey and John Absalom and several others, were going to pay off for the next generation of RIT hockey players. We had planted the seeds and helped nurture it to a point where it could blossom. So, we'd always feel a part of it. We still do, today."

• • •

The 1962–63 season would be a historic one for RIT hockey. Not only would the Tigers be playing home games at the Ritter-Clark Arena for the first time, but they also would be coached by a man who would receive a stipend from the university—making him the school's first paid hockey coach. Jim Heffer would lead the Tigers for six seasons, guiding them to 70 wins and only 27 losses and two ties. Pozefsky, who succeeded Allan Shepard as hockey club president, recalled how much it meant to have Heffer on board.

> We were grateful to Jack (Dykema) for donating his time to be our coach, but it was great to have a coach who was being paid by the school. It showed a further commitment to the program by the RIT administration. It was another step in us becoming legit.

Heffer was a technician in Eastman Kodak's photographic technology division who had been a successful youth hockey coach in the Rochester area. He was well respected for his knowledge of the sport, and his familiarity with the talent pool of young players in the region would aid him in recruiting. Jim was described by Tim Butler, who played four seasons of hockey at RIT before graduating in 1964, as "a rough-and-tumble kind of guy."

> Everybody loved him, especially the players and the student body. Jim was very spirited. On occasion, he would sit up in the stands, about three rows above the bench, and run the team from there. The students obviously loved that. There was one time when Jim decided to sit up with the cheerleaders and lead the crowd in cheers. I remember him not paying attention to the action and a puck flew over the boards and caught him right in the mouth. He wound up having to get a whole new set of front teeth as a result.

Heffer helped establish the program's winning tradition as his teams went 46–9–1 during one three-year stretch.

"Like I said, he was kind of rough around the edges,

Jim Heffer (left) was the first official RIT hockey coach, guiding the RIT men to a 70-27-2 record in six seasons.

and I think the university wanted to get somebody in place who was a little more professional," Butler said. "But Jim knew the game and he knew how to motivate you. I really liked playing for him, and the record speaks for itself."

In Heffer's coaching debut, Norm MacEachern from Toronto scored four goals and goalie Tom Frahm turned away 33 shots as RIT edged Hobart College, 8–6, at the

STORMIN' NORMAN, THE SCORING MACHINE

When describing the goal-scoring exploits of RIT forward Norm MacEachern in a March 1, 1963 article in *The Reporter*, the writer couldn't have been more effusive in his praise.

> Norm MacEachern of Toronto is so feared by opposing teams that he is usually double-teamed after the opening period of every game. Norm's slap-shot has pad-breaking speed and deadly accuracy which is seldom seen outside of professional hockey.

In this case, the hyperbole may have been justified, because the young RIT hockey program had never seen a scorer like MacEachern before. Though record-keeping was sketchy back then, he had at least five hat tricks—three or more goals in a single game—that season.

And the following year he was even better as his teammates voted him captain and the Tigers went 17–0–1, still the only unbeaten season in school history. MacEachern opened the 1963–64 campaign with a four-goal outburst in a 13–2 rout of Ithaca College. Midway through the season, he scored five goals in an 8–6 victory over Hamilton College. But MacEachern wound up saving his best for last, achieving a double hat trick—six goals—in the season-ending victory against Syracuse University on February 22, 1964. A half-century later, that school record still stands. Interestingly, though, it isn't an NCAA record. That mark belongs to Phil Latreille, who scored 10 goals for Middlebury College in a 1960 game against Colgate.

The RIT women's record is five goals, a feat achieved by Kim Eisenried in a January 9, 1985 game against Hamilton College and equaled by Kasie Strong in a January 19, 2002 game against MIT.

stuffed-to-the-rafters Ritter-Clark Arena. The Tigers wound up winning their first five games that season, including back-to-back contests against their crosstown rival, the University of Rochester, en route to a 7–3 record.

Having home games on campus proved to be a huge plus for RIT, as students routinely packed the 600-seat arena to capacity, and, occasionally, beyond.

"We had some games where people were sitting in the aisles," Pozefsky recalled. "I remember a few times when the Fire Marshall would come into the arena and ask people to leave because we were breaking all the fire codes. It was a cozy little bandbox of an arena, but that made for a fabulous atmosphere, and a pretty good home-ice advantage."

With a home to call its own, a $7,550 budget and a paid coach, the club was poised to take a quantum leap during the 1963–64 season, and it did. That team became the first and only team in RIT hockey history to go undefeated, posting a sterling 17–0–1 record. The only blemish was a 4–4 tie with Brockport, a game that still haunts members of that club till this day. "You sometimes wish you could go back in time and erase that game, but you can't," Butler said. "It's still pretty neat to think that in all the years they've been playing hockey at RIT and with all

The 1965-66 squad went 14–4–0, capping a three-year stretch when RIT posted a 46–9–1 record.

the great teams they've had, we still hold the distinction of being the only one that went unbeaten."

The Tigers outscored their opponents by an average of almost six goals per game. They clinched their first Finger Lakes Collegiate Hockey League title with a 10–2 thrashing of Syracuse University's club team at the New York State Fairgrounds Coliseum, north of Syracuse.

Perhaps, the most memorable moment of the season occurred on March 4, 1964, when MacEachern set a school record that still stands by scoring six goals in a single game to nip Syracuse, 10–7, at Ritter-Clark Arena. Between the first and second periods, RIT honored Rochesterian Janice Smith, a speed skater who had just returned from competing at the Winter Olympics in Innsbruck, Austria. The school presented her with a lifetime pass to all sporting events at RIT as well as an RIT varsity letter blanket. During intermission following the second period, Brockport's coach presented Heffer and co-captains Butler and MacEachern with the league title trophy his school had won the year before. That elicited thunderous applause from the packed house.

But an even bigger roar occurred a minute later when RIT Athletics Director Lou Alexander Jr. announced that hockey would officially become an intercollegiate sport during the 1964–65 season. Pozefsky described the team's feelings.

> It was a pretty emotional moment for all of us. We had been told a few years earlier it was going to happen, but I guess you don't really believe it until it becomes official. You think back on how far you've come.

Bill McLean, the high scorer on the '63–64 squad, recalled how, just two years earlier, a club from the University of Toronto had clobbered the Tigers, 23–0. "Marv was in goal that night and I thought he was going to go blind from the goal light flashing so much," McLean joked. "Of course, he didn't get much help from the rest of us. It was a total team effort. But you use such things as motivation and as measuring sticks. We had come a long, long way in a short period of time."

DEAF TRAILBLAZERS

Len Williams and Deane Sigler shared the dream of playing professional hockey someday. Though their fantasies were never realized, they did become pioneers at RIT, when, in 1972, they became the first NTID students to skate for the varsity.

And Williams added another "first" to his resume in 2004 when he became the first hockey player from NTID to be inducted into the RIT Sports Hall of Fame. From 1973 through '75, Williams scored 59 goals, including 37 in one season, a school record that stood for two decades. Three times, the Lake Placid, NY native scored five goals in a game, prompting his former coach, Daryl Sullivan, to say in a 2004 interview that Williams "was the best all-around player who ever skated for me." Williams continued to help his alma mater's hockey program after his playing career ended, serving as junior varsity and assistant varsity coach for four years. He wound up playing for the Deaf Olympics (Deaflympics) team in 1975 and 1979, and earned MVP honors after leading the team in scoring. He wound up landing tryouts with the Chicago Blackhawks of the National Hockey League and the Philadelphia Blazers of the World Hockey Association.

Sigler also competed in the Deaflympics, captaining the 1975 U.S. team. During his time with the Tigers, he established himself as a rugged defenseman capable of taking the puck up ice to score goals. He had 11 goals his first season and was second on the team in scoring his second season with 19. A member of the NTID Student Congress, Sigler helped the school host several tournaments at Ritter Arena for international deaf hockey teams.

Deane Sigler

Regina Russo was the first NTID student to play hockey for the RIT women. A native of White Plains, New York, where she attended the New York School for the Deaf, Russo played forward on the university's first women's team during the 1975–76 season. She had never played hockey before coming to RIT, but was an outstanding athlete with experience competing in swimming, track and field, baseball and basketball.

Coach Jim Heffer and his players from the 1966-67 team looking dapper in their suits and ties.

Indeed, they had. From scrounging to find enough players to field a municipal league team in 1957 to having to cut more than half of the 45 players who tried out in 1963. From 23–0 thumpings to 13–0 victories like the one they scored against Niagara during their unbeaten season. From playing their entire schedule on the road to having a rink of their own. "Thinking back on the journey," Butler said, "you couldn't help but feel a sense of immense pride."

WILLOW
EUROPEAN
FIESTA
TEN FOX
FOXTROT
ROCKER
Cooper

2.

LAUNCHING THE WOMEN'S PROGRAM

The idea of forming a women's hockey team began percolating in Sheila Stevenson's brain not long after she arrived on campus as a freshman in the fall of 1975. Growing up in Canton, New York, not far from the Canadian border, Stevenson became interested in hockey after tagging along to her older brothers' practices and games. The boys let her play in some of their pickup games on the neighborhood ponds, and she took to the sport immediately. Many North Country girls shared her passion for the sport, and it wasn't long before organized girls' leagues featuring town teams began sprouting. In a 2014 interview, Stevenson outlined the progression of female involvement in the sport.

> I guess we were ahead of the curve as far as organized girls' hockey was concerned. Hockey was big in our region because of our proximity to Canada and our long winters. A lot of us started out by playing with the boys in our neighborhoods. And as we got older there was a large enough number of girls who wanted to continue playing, and that's when they started up all-girls town teams in places like Canton and Potsdam and Messina. We'd play games against each other and also play in a lot of tournaments against Canadian teams. It was a lot of fun, and the competition was very good.

When Stevenson came to RIT, she was disappointed to discover there wasn't a women's team. To sate her appetite for the game, she enrolled in a physical education hockey course taught by RIT men's coach Daryl Sullivan. "I vividly remember going to the gym to sign up for the class and there was this guy making some snide remark about this not being a figure-skating class," she said. "I wanted to check him into the boards, but I just kept my mouth shut." Stevenson's skating and stick-handling abilities immediately impressed Sullivan. After several classes, Stevenson broached the idea of forming a women's club team, and Sullivan encouraged her to meet with athletics director Lou Alexander Jr., who said she could pursue the idea. Alexander told her that the school couldn't provide any financial support, but would offer the team free practice time at Ritter

Opposite: Paula Hoffman was the first goalie in RIT women's hockey history.

RIT students, wearing figure skates, participate in a practice hockey game at the Ritter-Clark Arena on the downtown campus in the early 1960s.

Arena. "He said if we could prove that there was enough interest, the school might consider supporting us the following season," said Stevenson, who went on to have a distinguished career as a sports information director at Rowan University in Glassboro, New Jersey. "But it was clear that the onus would fall solely on us to get the thing launched. The school gave us free ice time, but not much else. I contacted some of my former town-team teammates who were playing women's hockey at places like St. Lawrence and Cortland, just to pick their brains. I figured they could give me some advice because they were members of established programs."

The first challenge would be the recruitment of enough like-minded women to field a team. Stevenson posted notices in academic buildings and dormitories throughout campus and also received a boost from sports information director Roger Dykes, who ran blurbs about the formation of the team in the men's game-day hockey leaflets as well as in the student newspaper, *The Reporter*. "It was pretty much word-of-mouth," Stevenson said. "I had no idea what kind of interest there would be, but I wanted to continue playing hockey, so it was worth a shot to me." The first organizational meeting that fall attracted 18 women. The vast majority of them had never played organized hockey before, and there were a few who barely knew how to skate. "I was encouraged by the turnout," Stevenson said. "It was great to see that we had a number of women who had excelled in other sports, so I was hopeful that some of their skills would be transferable to the ice."

Among the women with other sports experience were senior defenseman Mel Cameron, who had played varsity tennis and volleyball at RIT; freshman wing Dorothea Derke, a high school all-star in field hockey and volleyball; sophomore wing Regina Russo (swimming, track, softball and basketball); freshman center Nancie Lewis (field hockey); junior forward Carmella Cornaccio (track and field), and junior forward Beth Laasko (manager of the RIT men's hockey team). "We were a rag-tag bunch, to be sure," said Paula Hoffman McGinnis, the goalie on that charter team. "But everyone seemed enthused about the opportunity to give hockey a try. I know I was."

Freshman Dich Gordon, who had experience playing intramural hockey, also attended the meeting. He volunteered to coach the team, along with his roommate, Dave Ziegelhofer. "That was great because it took a big load off my shoulders," said Stevenson, who served as the team's captain. "They were extremely helpful, especially when it came to running practices and games." Laura Oakley Beebe, a freshman forward on the original team,

Sheila Stevenson (left), the founder of the RIT women's hockey program, poses with teammate Kris VanValkenburg (right).

said she and her teammates were grateful to Gordon and Ziegelhofer for donating their time.

"We almost always practiced late at night (usually from 11 p.m.–midnight), so that was a huge sacrifice on their part. We had a lot of girls who didn't know how to skate very well and Dich and Dave never lost their patience with us. They were always very encouraging, very upbeat."

Hoffman McGinnis admitted to feeling a bit of trepidation at first. She had attended an all-girls Catholic high school in Reston, Virginia, and by her own admission "wasn't very athletic" but was intrigued by the idea of playing hockey.

> I lived in Michigan until I was eight years old, and I remember how my brothers had played hockey and how jealous I was because they got to attend (National Hockey League legend) Gordie Howe's hockey camp. I'd always loved hockey. When I got to RIT I was interested in trying new stuff. It was a club team, not a varsity team, so I thought it was something I might be able to do. I knew I had to improve my skating, so I took a skating class as one of my gym electives. One of the things that really helped me from that class is that I learned how to skate backwards.

That skill would come in handy when the junior fine arts and photographic illustration major decided to become a netminder because goalies do a lot of backwards skating.

> A lot of the girls that showed up wanted to play forward or center—the positions where you

PIONEERING WOMEN	NAME	POS.	YR.	HOMETOWN
Founded and captained by Sheila Stevenson and coached by Dich Gordon and Dave Ziegelhofer, the RIT women's hockey team lost both of its games during its inaugural season in 1975–76. Here are the members of that first women's squad:	Sheila Stevenson	D	Fr.	Canton, NY
	Paula Hoffman	G	Jr.	Reston, VA
	Regina Russo	W	So.	White Plains, NY
	Laura Oakley	W	Fr.	Guilderland, NY
	Pat Hogan	C	Sr.	Clarence, NY
	Dorothea Derke	W	Fr.	Franklin, NY
	Nancie Lewis	C	Fr.	Auburn, NY
	Mel Cameron	D	Sr.	Buffalo, NY
	Carmella Cornacchio	W	Jr.	Elmira, NY
	Beth Laasko	W	Jr.	Huntington Beach, CA
	Diana Thompson	W	Fr.	Cuyahoga Falls, OH
	Kathy Good	W	Fr.	Silver Springs, MD

> could skate down the ice and score goals. Skating wasn't my strong suit, so I said to myself, "Why don't I just play goalie? I won't have to work as much because I won't be skating up and down the ice and it will be safer because I'll be all padded up with protective equipment." Foolish me. I quickly discovered that playing in net is a heckuva lot of work and it isn't so safe having pucks fired at you. What was I thinking?

Procuring equipment was also challenging. The women received a bunch of tattered, hand-me-down gloves, protective padding, sticks and pucks from the men's team, brothers, and boyfriends. But, for the most part, they were on their own and forced to shell out their own money in order to cobble together the necessary equipment needed to suit up.

"I was given some old shin guards—I don't know where they came from, but they were too small," Hoffman McGinnis recalled. "Luckily, there was a guy in my dorm who was selling his old goalie pads. They were pretty beat up, but they were in decent shape and they fit me, so I bought the set for about $50. I inherited a mitt from the men's team and went out and bought a waffle glove. I got a chest protector from the catcher on the baseball team. That spring I wound up buying a pair of used goalie skates—I didn't even know until then that goalies wore different kinds of skates. I also bought a boy's athletic supporter and cup, because I was told I would need to protect my private areas. My teammates got a laugh out of that, but it did serve its purpose because I got hit down there a few times."

For jerseys, Stevenson went to a local sporting goods factory outlet and bought a bunch of oversized, plain-colored sweatshirts. As a school project, students in her screenprinting class emblazoned "R.I.T." on the front

Liz Dopp, a forward with the team from 1979–83, helped spearhead changes that resulted in improved equipment, ice time and transportation for the women's team.

of the sweatshirts. "Everything else we wore was hodge-podge, but at least everyone had the same colored jersey on, so we at least *looked* like a team," Stevenson said, chuckling.

Thanks to some of her contacts, Stevenson was able to convince the women's teams at Cortland State and St. Lawrence to come to Ritter Arena to play games. On March 5, 1976, after weeks of practices and intra-squad scrimmages, RIT women's hockey played its first game ever, against the Cortland Red Dragons at Ritter Arena.

"I really don't remember much about the game," Laura Oakley Beebe said. "All I remember is being nervous and excited. We all were anxious to see how we would fare against another team."

Oakley Beebe and company wound up acquitting themselves well in a 5–2 loss in front of a couple hundred enthusiastic fans. Stevenson, appropriately enough, scored the first goal in RIT women's hockey history at 11:43 of the first period. Dorothea Derke scored the other goal. This duo would wind up leading the way for the Tigers during their first four seasons. Goalie Hoffman McGinnis thought that first game went reasonably well.

> It was a pretty good start considering we were the newcomers and we had several girls who not only had never played hockey before, but could barely stand up on the ice. We received decent support from our fellow students. Our friends and boyfriends showed up, as well as a bunch of curiosity seekers who wanted to see what women's hockey was all about.

What they saw was a game different from the men's game. Periods were 15 rather than 20 minutes long. Body checks and slap shots weren't permitted. "I could be wrong, but I want to say it was running time, meaning the clock wasn't stopped if the puck went up into the

Lori Farr, a 1983 professional photography graduate, tallied 26 goals and 23 assists during her hockey career at RIT. In 2011, she and her husband, David Rusin, a former Tigers assistant head coach, donated $50,000 to establish the Ruth Corcoran Hockey Endowment Fund in memory of the woman who was regarded as an unofficial "team mother."

stands," Hoffman McGinnis said. "That probably was a good thing because a shorter game meant fewer goals by the opposing team." The only other game that season was played at Ritter seven nights later as St. Lawrence scored a decisive 8–3 victory. "I thought we were fairly competitive in both games," Stevenson said. "And, although we lost each one, we had gotten the thing off the ground enough to convince the administration that we deserved to be a fully supported club team the next season."

The founder of the women's hockey team came up with a budget for equipment and travel, and the RIT athletics department helped arrange an 11-game schedule for the 1976–77 season. Eight players returned from the charter team and eight new women joined to boost the roster to 16, four more than the previous season. Gordon returned as coach and was assisted by Skip Blicker, a member of the RIT men's varsity hockey team. Sports Information Director Roger Dykes continued providing his support by compiling a media brochure and game programs, and sending out press releases, just as he did for each of the school's varsity sports.

Despite the strides the players had made, the second season of RIT women's hockey would emphatically underscore the wide talent gap between their fledgling program and the established programs. The Tigers wound up going 0–10–1, their only non-loss coming in a 1–1 overtime tie with Clarkson University in the season finale. Not only would they go winless, but they would be outscored 84–12. The season got off to a terrible start with a December 8, 1976 visit to Ithaca to play Cornell University. The Big Red obliterated RIT, 21–0, peppering Hoffman McGinnis with 62 shots on goal. She remembers it well.

> I'll never forget taking the ice against them. As they did their pre-game skate, I couldn't get over how big they were. Those girls were like Amazons. I remember being very sore and tired after that game and going into the locker room and seeing these glazed looks on everyone's face. It was a long, long night.

A PROFILE IN COURAGE

After receiving the devastating news on December 2, 1996 that she had Hodgkin's disease, Kristine Pierce didn't have to look far to find a source of strength and inspiration. In the years leading up to her diagnosis, the RIT hockey player had watched her father handle his struggles with a rare and painful liver disease with grace and dignity.

"I think I adopted his attitude when I was facing my problems," she said. "What he went through was so much more threatening and challenging than what I faced. I figured if he could get through that, I could get past my little Hodgkin's hurdle."

Her challenge was hardly little—there were many painful moments as she endured nausea, neck burns, hair loss and uncertainty during months of chemotherapy and radiation treatments. But the positive attitude her father modeled for her would serve her well, and nine months later, she was declared cancer-free.

Pierce returned to the ice with a greater appreciation and passion for hockey—and for life. During and after her illness, she immersed herself in community service, volunteering for 27 different organizations, including Big Brothers, Big Sisters, Habitat for Humanity, Camp Good Days and Special Times and a local soup kitchen. As captain of the hockey team, she also encouraged her teammates to join her in community service projects.

"Hodgkin's changed my life forever," she said, at the time. "At first, I was angry with God for doing this to me, but I came to understand that it was the best thing that could have happened to me. I have come to realize that there are so many less fortunate people in this world . . . What's important to me now is putting smiles on people's faces, helping those in need or making a difference in this ever-changing world."

Kristine Pierce

Pierce's immense compassion, along with her hockey prowess and academic excellence, did not go unnoticed. In 1999, the All-American defenseman became the first woman and the first Division III athlete to receive the Hockey Humanitarian Award, which is presented annually to college hockey's "finest citizen." Pierce's remarkable story was featured, along with those about icons Michael Jordan, Wayne Gretzky and John Elway, in a special "Heroes Edition" of *Sport* magazine. At commencement ceremonies after receiving her degree in hotel management in May 1999, Pierce was asked to stand up. She was given a thunderous ovation.

That December, in ceremonies before a men's hockey game between RIT and Elmira at Ritter Arena, Pierce achieved another first when she became the first and only athlete in school history to have a jersey number retired. Her No. 12 hangs in a plaque inside the new Polessini Center. In 2007, Pierce was inducted into the RIT Sports Hall of Fame.

"We are very happy and honored for Kristine," said Lou Spiotti, the school's athletics director. "I have seen thousands of student athletes pass through our program. Kristine will stay in our memories as the one who had the most positive impact."

Though there would be two other routs by 10 goals, RIT never quit, and came within a goal or two of winning three games. Despite being bombarded with shots throughout the season, Hoffman McGinnis held her own, making 220 saves along the way. Derke led RIT with five goals and two assists for seven points, while freshmen Kathy Good and Nancie Lewis added two goals apiece. The team also featured Jan Bakken, a 27-year-old mother who joined the squad halfway through the first season.

Hoffman McGinnis's hockey career had ended without her tasting victory, but she said she has no regrets in retrospect.

> Some of my fondest RIT memories were my two seasons playing hockey. The camaraderie we enjoyed and just knowing that I was the first goalie in school history made it an exceptional experience. We were underdogs and weren't expected to win, so I think we had less pressure on us and we could be a little freer to have fun. We all feel a special sense of pride that we got it off the ground, and it was all because of Sheila. She was definitely the driving force.

The program took a big step in the fall of 1977 when athletic director Bill Carey announced women's hockey would become a varsity sport. He hired Bob Green to be the head coach and Dich Gordon stayed on as an assistant. Five veterans, including Stevenson and Derke, returned and were joined by 11 newcomers, including six freshmen. Despite the elevation in status, the Tigers continued to take their lumps, being outscored 41–5 in their first five games, all losses. But as the season progressed, they became more competitive. Although they lost their next three, they were outscored by just a 13–9 margin. They concluded their first varsity season with a 3–3 tie against the University of Rochester to finish 0–8–1.

The 1978–79 campaign would be the fourth and final season for charter members Stevenson, Nancie Lewis, Dorothea Derke and Dich Gordon. Each had played a pivotal role in starting and nurturing RIT women's hockey, and their persistence would be rewarded that winter as they finished their puck careers on a high note. That season would feature the program's first victory—a 5–3 win against Brockport State in the season opener—and RIT's first winning record, 6–4. Each of the wins came on home ice. Derke, a senior forward from Franklin, New York, established records for most goals in a game (3), season (9) and career (24), while Lewis, a center, established marks for most assists in a game (3), season (7) and career (14). Although Stevenson didn't record a goal or assist that season and finished her 32-game career with just a goal and three assists, her true value as a four-year defenseman and captain was immeasurable. Her efforts in guiding the Tigers to their first winning record made her a finalist for the school's woman athlete of the year award. In 2005, Stevenson was inducted into RIT's Athletic Hall of Fame. Eight years later, she received the Warren Berg Award, the highest honor bestowed by the College Sports Information Directors Association. Stevenson is proud that her alma mater's hockey program has achieved national recognition, but continues to downplay the role she had in forming the team.

> I might have been the one to get it going, but I don't view myself as a pioneer. In reality, I consider all the women who played on those first teams as the founding mothers of RIT hockey. There isn't just one.

The 1984-85 team won 80 percent of its games, a school record that would stand for 22 years.

361
DBOOST

3.

WINNING IT ALL IN 1983

When Brian Mason was introduced to the Rochester media as RIT's new men's hockey coach in 1980, he boldly predicted that the Tigers would be nationally recognized by the end of his four-year contract. As it turned out, he wound up delivering on his promise a year ahead of schedule. On March 19, 1983, the Tigers hockey team went where no RIT sports team had gone before by winning the first national championship in the university's 154-year history. Their improbable 4–2 victory over Bemidji State in the NCAA Division II title game in Billerica, Massachusetts, capped an improbable season that saw the Tigers open with three consecutive losses and suffer a shocking upset defeat in the first round of the ECAC tournament that cast a doubt over whether they would even receive an invitation to the NCAAs. In the end, though, they did, and they made the most of it. "We began that season dreaming about winning it all," said goalie and team most valuable player Dave Burkholder. "And our dreams came true."

• • •

An Ottawa native, Mason was just 32 years old when he took over the program from his predecessor, Daryl Sullivan. What he lacked in age, he more than made up for in hockey experience and expertise. Mason had been an outstanding junior hockey player who earned a scholarship to Clarkson University, leading the collegiate hockey powerhouse in scoring in his junior and senior years. Following his graduation in 1973, Mason signed a professional contract with the Dayton Gems of the International Hockey League. Shortly after the start of his third pro season, Mason was driven to the ice by a check and wound up dislocating his right shoulder and suffering partial paralysis that lasted nearly six months. He attempted a comeback, but his shoulder kept acting up. After 14 dislocations requiring three operations, he finally acquiesced and retired from playing. Wanting to stay involved in the sport, Mason landed a job coaching the Northwood Prep School team in Lake Placid. He thoroughly enjoyed imparting his vast knowledge of the game to young men, and his teams responded by dominating their opponents. In 1978, Mason became an assistant at Rensselaer Polytechnic Institute, a Division I school near

Opposite: Members of RIT's 1982-83 national championship team make a triumphant return to campus.

Albany, and he continued to shine.

RIT's search for a coach attracted 50–60 applicants and none of them, in athletic director Lou Spiotti's mind, was a better fit than Mason. "Mason impressed me with his coaching confidence, his understanding of the game, his background and his student priorities," Spiotti said. "He was the right type we wanted for the student-athlete at RIT." Although it wasn't required of him, Mason also insisted on teaching some physical education courses at the school. "I figured it would be a good way for me to stay in touch with the students," he said. "I thought that was important as I tried to take the program to another level."

Mason's coaching career at RIT got off to a bumpy start, as the team lost its first three games and five of its first seven. A stickler for discipline and hustle, Mason cut five players, including two top-scoring veterans and a defenseman he had recruited. "There was a lack of commitment," he explained. "It was no big deal . . . I simply

DARYL SULLIVAN – RIT'S FIRST FULL-TIME COACH

Daryl Sullivan's players fondly remember him as "Boots" because he wore old-fashioned rubber boots with buckles on them whenever he was at the rink. But the former RIT men's hockey coach's choice of footwear wasn't the only thing that made a lasting impression on them. "He was a lot of fun to play for," recalled Marty Reeners of the man who coached the Tigers from 1968–80, leading them to two Finger Lakes Collegiate Hockey League titles and three Eastern Collegiate Athletic Conference championship games. "I learned a lot from him. In fact, many of the coaching techniques I wound up employing were things 'Boots' Sullivan taught me."

A native of Potsdam, New York, not far from the Canadian border, Sullivan transferred after two years at Clarkson University to play for RIT Coach Jim Heffer. After receiving a degree in electrical engineering in 1965, he became Heffer's assistant. When Heffer retired three years later, Sullivan became the first full-time hockey coach in school history, and also worked as an RIT physical education instructor. It was a momentous time for the program because 1968 marked the first year the Tigers played at Frank Ritter Arena on the then-new suburban campus in Henrietta, New York. Sullivan's first season wound up being his best, as RIT finished 17–9–1. He would lead the Tigers to double-digit victory seasons six times, compiling a 131–135–3 mark.

Along the way, he coached several outstanding players, including forwards Dennis Lepley, Ken Vokac, Ron Kerr (RIT's first ECAC Rookie of the Year), Len Williams, Doug Heffer (son of Jim Heffer), Norm Reid, Rick Kozlowski, Al Vyverberg, Jay Hill and Reeners; defensemen Deane Sigler, Mike Meyer, Terry Lantry and Glenn Howarth; and goaltenders Jim Blaise, Mark Dougherty and Marty Reasoner. Sullivan resigned his coaching position after 12 years to become the university's coordinator of intramurals. However, he still kept his hand in hockey, serving as an off-ice official at all men's home games. He was inducted into the RIT Sports Hall of Fame in 1992.

The 1982-83 team established a then-school-record with 23 wins, a mark they would surpass the following season.

replaced them with kids who wanted to work." After the message of tough love was delivered, the Tigers won nine of 10 and finished the season with a 14–10 record. Though that was only a two-game improvement over the previous season, Mason had laid the foundation for the future, and from that point on proved to be a skilled recruiter. The Tigers made a big jump in 1981–82, posting a 21–10–1 record. The stage was set for a national championship season. "Even when we were doing dry land training before we even set foot on ice for the '82–'83 campaign, you could tell something special was brewing," said Chris Johnstone, a center on those teams. "It felt like the kind of team that could make a run."

The run, though, would start with a stumble—three losses by a total of just four goals. The Tigers quickly righted themselves, winning eight of their next nine before losing to two-time defending national champion Lowell, 5–3, at the Joe Tully Fan Forum in Billerica, Massachusetts..

"We lost it on our power plays," defenseman Ed Carroll said of the Tigers' failure to capitalize on man-up situations following Lowell penalties. "But we came away from that game knowing that we could play with those guys on their home ice. They were the standard-bearers and we figured we'd be seeing them down the road again, so that was significant."

RIT responded with another streak in which it won 12 of its next 14 to finish the regular season at 20–7 and earn the top seed and home-ice advantage for the Eastern Collegiate Athletic Conference tournament. "We were

A TIGER AT THE OLYMPICS

Occasionally, Marty Reeners will reflect on how much differently his life would have turned out had Coach Daryl Sullivan decided to fill RIT's last roster spot with someone else.

> It came down to me and one other kid—Kevin Klossman—and Daryl, for some reason, went with me," said Reeners, who graduated in 1974 with a degree in printing management. " If I had gotten cut, I never would have played hockey at RIT, wouldn't have met my wife, wouldn't have had three kids who are still playing hockey as adults, and I wouldn't have stayed involved in the game the way I did.

A few years after playing his last game for the Tigers, Reeners embarked on a 32-year career as a hockey referee that saw him work games at the youth, college and professional levels, including the American Hockey League, just a step below the NHL. The pinnacle of his career occurred when he was selected to work the 1980 Winter Olympics in Lake Placid. Those, of course, were the "Miracle on Ice" Olympics, when the ragtag U.S. hockey team stunned the mighty Soviet Union squad en route to a gold medal. In those days, referees weren't allowed to work games featuring their home country, so Reeners instead officiated contests involving other countries, such as Czechoslovakia, Finland, Sweden and Canada. His credentials did allow him to witness all but one of the U.S. games—an early-round contest against Germany.

Marty Reeners

Reeners had hoped to work in the NHL, and actually officiated some exhibition games, but the call-up never came. "No regrets," he said. "I'm just thankful Daryl gave me a shot way back when, because hockey wound up giving me so much."

all sure we were going to win," Carroll said of that first-round matchup against No. 8 seed Middlebury College. But overconfidence and complacency got the better of them, and the Tigers were bounced from the tournament with a stunning 5–3 loss. Suddenly, RIT's hopes of receiving a bid to the NCAA Division II tournament were in jeopardy. Johnstone recalled the team's nerves.

> We sweated out the next week. We thought we might get the eighth seed if we were lucky. Every day that following week I'd come up to Coach (Mason) and ask, "Are we in? Are we in?"

Five days after being upset by Middlebury, he finally received his answer. Yes, the Tigers were in. As the fifth seed, they would host Mankato State in a two-game, total goal series, meaning the team that had more goals after two games would advance to the following week's Final Four.

In front of a packed Ritter Arena, the Tigers won that Friday night's opener in impressive fashion, 6–1. That meant they would begin the next evening's game with a seemingly insurmountable five-goal advantage. But Mankato State made things interesting by scoring the first four goals.

"We were starting to panic a little," Johnstone recalled. "The momentum clearly had shifted and they were making a charge. At that point, I just told the guys, 'Hey, we're still up by a goal. Let's settle down and regroup and let's treat this thing like it's a 2–1 game and we're ahead.'"

And that's what they did, scoring three of the next five goals. Although they lost, 6–3, they had won the two-game series, nine goals to seven, and had punched their ticket to their first Final Four.

Chris Johnstone, who played on two national championship teams in the 1980s, remains the school's all-time goal scorer (114) and points leader (250).

It just so happened that their semifinal match would be against mighty Lowell on its home rink. The Chiefs had lost just one game all season—to Division I power RPI. Lowell had won the previous two Division II national championships and was preparing to become a Division I program the next season. Most expected the top-seeded Chiefs to make easy work of the upstart Tigers.

But RIT had a couple of things working in its

favor. First, there was the December 19th game in which the Tigers had pretty much held their own against Lowell. Second, the haughty Chiefs provided some additional incentive at the banquet feting the four teams the night before the semifinals. RIT goalie Dave Burkholder said the Chiefs' championship rings stoked his team's competitive spirit.

"It was hard not to notice those rings. It gave us some additional motivation, for sure. They had their rings. We wanted to get some of our own."

When the Tigers took the ice for their semifinal game against Lowell, Johnstone and his teammates felt quite calm.

"We're in a hostile environment, playing the biggest game of our lives, and I couldn't believe how relaxed I felt," Johnstone said. "We should have been nervous as hell, but we weren't. We all seemed so poised. To me, that was a great sign. The pressure was all on them to three-peat. We were the underdogs. We were as loose as can be."

It showed. Chuck Samar scored two goals and Johnstone and Bobby Trowell also scored as RIT knocked off the heavy favorites, 4–1. But the big star was someone who prevented goals rather than scoring them. Despite facing relentless pressure, Burkholder turned away 43 of 44 shots fired at the RIT goal. Early in the game, he gloved a point-blank shot from Lowell's All-American center, Mike Carr. After the save, Carr skated toward the crease and told Burkholder: "You're (bleeping) lucky." The young man who'd been playing goalie since he was five just laughed.

Before the game, Mason had told reporters and his team that "to win this game, we don't need average goaltending; we need *great* goaltending." Burkholder clearly was up for the challenge.

Although the Tigers had stunned the college hockey world, their work wasn't done. Bemidji, their opponent in the title game, was the tournament's second seed and featured a fast-skating, high-scoring lineup. Burkholder would be tested again. Numerous times. And he would ace the test once more.

He denied 30 of Bemidji's 32 shots as RIT scored a 4–2 victory in the biggest game to that point in school history. Johnstone got the Tigers off on the right foot when he scored 59 seconds into the game. Bemidji tied the score near the end of the first period. Mason could sense that his team was tight. In the locker room during the first intermission, he told his players: "This team's not as good as you guys. Let's loosen it up and get it going."

Samar scored on an assist from Trowell one minute into the second period to put RIT back on top. Freshman center Mike Holzman and sophomore wing Rich Brouwer scored before the midway point of the final period to boost the Tigers lead to 4–1. With just over nine minutes

Goalie Dave Burkholder was the most valuable player at the 1983 NCAA Division III Final Four.

Teammates hug goalie Dave Burkholder after he turned away 30 of 32 shots in a 4-2 victory against Bemidji in the 1983 title game.

remaining, Bemidji's All-American center Joel Otto beat Burkholder to close the gap to two goals. At that point Burkholder gave himself a talking-to.

> I was a little worried. But I regrouped and told myself, 'Okay, Burk, settle down. Get back to concentrating and grind out this victory.'

He denied Bemidji's swarming attack the rest of the way. There was a brief play stoppage with 33 seconds remaining. Carroll, who was on the bench, paused and gazed up at the scoreboard. The enormousness of the moment finally hit him. "Oh my God," he said, "we're going to be national champions."

When the horn sounded ending the game, Carroll and his benchmates leapt onto the ice and began skating toward Burkholder, who was engulfed by teammates already on the ice. Mason shook hands with his assistants, then bit his lip and tried not to cry. After several minutes of celebrating on the ice, the RIT players skated back to the bench and Mason exchanged hugs and high-fives with each of them. About 500 RIT fans who had made the trip to Lowell's Joe Tully Forum began chanting, "R!I!T!" "Take it all in," Mason reminded his players just before the awards ceremony began. "It may never happen again."

Johnstone, Samar and senior defenseman Mark Burgholzer skated out to receive their All-Tournament team trophies. They were followed by Burkholder, who

Members of the Tigers proclaim themselves No. 1 after championship victory.

to no one's surprise had been named the tournament's most valuable player. The RIT fans chanted, "Burkie! Burkie! Burkie!" as the man who had turned away 73 shots in two games hoisted his award above his head.

"We came here with a dream—all of us," Burkholder said. "We believed we could win the national championship. We knew we were good enough."

The biggest cheer was reserved for the presentation of national championship trophy. As Mason and his players posed for photographs with the award at center ice, RIT president Richard Rose studied the jubilant scene and fought back tears.

"Parents, students, alumni and faculty can be proud of and enjoy this achievement," Rose told a reporter. "It's an emotional moment. I'm happy for Brian, for the team, for the city, and everyone involved.

In the media interviews that followed, Burkholder showered praise on his teammates, Mason, and assistant coach Jim Pettie, who was a former professional goalie with the Rochester Americans. Mason, arms hugging the championship trophy as if it were a child, smiled as he told reporters how this all came to be.

> We went out and got quality kids and we worked and we worked and we worked. We worked so hard that I know my personal life has suffered. I'm taking my wife on a vacation next week—the coaches' convention in Sarasota (Florida).

RIT player John Hinrichsen presents a framed photo of the championship ring to president Richard Rose.

Mason then talked about Burkholder's enormous contributions.

> It was a great team effort, but Burkie was the leader. He inspired the entire team. He simply dared everybody to put the puck past him.

The following day the team bused back to RIT for a rally. At New York State Thruway Exit 46 in Henrietta, just a few miles south of campus, the team bus was met by several patrol cars from the Monroe County Sheriff's Department to give them an escort. "When we turned into the circle at the administration building and saw all those students and other people there waiting to greet us, I had to fight back the tears," Mason said.

As an estimated crowd of almost 1,500 looked on, Spiotti, Mason, Rose, Burkholder and other school officials delivered several short speeches. The instant Rose mentioned the words "national championship" while handing the NCAA plaque to Mason, there was thunderous applause.

"He coached a perfect weekend at this tournament,"-said Spiotti. "There may have been more talent on other teams, but Coach Mason got more out of our players than the other coaches got out of theirs. They played inspired hockey and that was a tribute to Brian."

The national championship only enhanced recruiting. With a few highly touted newcomers arriving to go

Coach Brian Mason (holding trophy) is hoisted on his players' shoulders during campus celebration.

Players parade the NCAA championship trophy around campus.

with a core of returning players, RIT was the favorite to repeat its crown—this time at the Division III level. The drop one level made sense because RIT didn't give out scholarships, so it would be more in line in Division III, where athletic scholarships are prohibited. Like the season before, the Tigers stumbled out of the gate, this time losing four straight, though each of the losses came at the hands of Division I programs, including a 3–0 loss to Mason's alma mater, Clarkson University. The games against the top level of college hockey served the Tigers well, because after opening 0–4, they reeled off 17 consecutive victories. After suffering a streak-snapping 5–4 loss at Oswego, RIT won 11 more in a row.

Unfortunately, the Tigers' next loss would end not only their win streak, but also their dreams for a second NCAA title. By exacting revenge on Oswego with convincing 13–2 and 10–1 wins in the opening rounds of the NCAA tournament, the Tigers won the right to host the 1984 Final Four at Ritter Arena. Their semifinal game against Union College would be one of the most memorable and painful in RIT hockey history as they lost, 5–4, in four overtimes in front of a standing-room-only crowd of 2,100. Gill Egan scored the game-winner three minutes and 26 seconds into the fourth extra session when he rifled a 30-foot slap shot over Burkholder's glove hand. The goal brought an emphatic end to a marathon game that took 93 minutes and 26 seconds to decide. There weren't any shoot-out rules in effect, as there are today, so the teams played on through three 20-minute regulation periods and three 10-minute overtimes, plus the three minutes and 26 seconds of the fourth extra session.

The way the game began, it didn't appear any extra periods would be needed. Freshman right wing Ritchie Herbert, the first black player in RIT hockey history, scored twice in the first five minutes and 22 seconds as the Tigers raced to a 2–0 lead. But Union stormed back, tying the game in the second period on goals by Joe Picano and John MacKenzie. Less than a minute after MacKenzie's game-tying goal, Johnstone tapped in a rebound to give the Tigers a 3–2 lead. But Egan, who had spent the previous day in the RIT infirmary with a severe cold, knotted the score when he pushed the puck past Burkholder with less than two minutes remaining in the second period.

Seven minutes into the final period of regulation, the Tigers regained the lead once more as Brouwer scored

COMING UP SHORT IN THE LONGEST GAME

The luck of the Irish wasn't with the RIT hockey team on St. Patrick's Day in 1984 as Gill Egan slapped a shot past RIT goalie Dave Burkholder to give Union College a 5–4 victory in four overtimes in the NCAA Division III semifinals before a stunned standing-room-only crowd of 2,100 in Ritter Arena. The goal put an end to the Tigers' dreams of a second consecutive national championship. It also ended a rivetingly exhausting game that had seen the teams battle through three 20-minute periods, three 10-minute overtime periods, and three minutes and 26 seconds into a fourth overtime.

It was the longest game in RIT history and the longest college hockey game ever played to that point. Interestingly, a few weeks later Bowling Green University would break the record by playing a four-overtime game that lasted 97 minutes, 11 seconds—three minutes and 45 seconds longer than the RIT–Union game. Bowling Green's 5–4 victory over Minnesota–Duluth enabled it to win the NCAA Division I national championship. The captain of that title team was Wayne Wilson, who 15 years later would become RIT's head coach.

The longest game in college hockey history occurred on March 12, 2010, when Quinnipiac defeated Union, 3–2, in a five-overtime contest that took 150 minutes and 22 seconds to complete. The Division III record is a February 27, 2010 game between Gustavus Adolphus and Augsburg that lasted 138 minutes and 38 seconds.

A PLUCK FOR STOPPING PUCKS

During their days as RIT hockey goalies, Marty Reasoner, Jocelyn Guimond, Laurie Davis and Ali Binnington learned what it's like to be shooting range targets and what it's like to be the person who saves the day. Despite facing a relentless barrage of shots on goal, these four netminders blocked, caught and kicked their way into the hockey record books.

In a 7–6 victory against Canton on March 6, 1974, Reasoner turned away a school-record 74 shots. Remarkably, there have been seven performances in NCAA Division III hockey annals when a goalie has recorded more saves, topped by the 98 made by Justin Lochner of Augsburg (Minnesota) College against Gustavus Adolphus College on February 27, 2010. Reasoner, who also played wing early in his RIT career and once scored the winning goal in overtime, had another game where he made 66 saves in a 7–6 overtime loss at heavily favored Oswego.

"I swear the stat crew's bookkeeping was off in that game because I had more like 76 saves in regulation and at least another 10 in overtime before Oswego scored the game-winner against me," Reasoner said. "So, it was probably more like 85 or 86 saves, but who's counting? When you are getting peppered with that many shots, it's hard for the statisticians to keep up."

Oswego was the far superior team, with several Canadian players, but Reasoner kept the Tigers in contention until the bitter end. "They kept coming at me in waves," he recalled. "A reporter said it was like the rink was tilted 10 degrees toward me and they were skating downhill against us." Despite those scintillating performances, Reasoner's greatest hockey contribution may have been his son of the same name who went on to play 13 seasons in the NHL.

Jocelyn Guimond

Guimond's seminal game

a power play goal. But Joe Caruso's goal at 16:17 of the third tied the score at 4, and when neither team was able to light the lamp in the remaining three-plus minutes, the game went into overtime. And then, another overtime. And another. And another, before Egan scored his second goal of the night to snap RIT's 11-game win streak and chances for another title. Burkholder, who would finish his career with a sterling 104–36–1 record, took the loss hard. "It's my fault," he said. "He just blew it by me. I lost it for these guys." It was one of the few games during his career when the two-time ECAC goaltender of the year was outplayed by his fellow netminder. Union's Wayne McDougall finished with 51 saves to Burkholder's 36. Mason told the *Democrat and Chronicle*,

> Sometimes it's just not in the books for you. Give Union credit. They played well. Their goaltender was tremendous and we couldn't get a goal. We didn't have anything left at the end.

occurred on October 26, 2006, when he made 66 saves in a 3–2 victory over St. Lawrence University. Although the Division I record for saves is 78, by Dick Greenlawn of Rensselaer Polytechnic Institute, Guimond's total tied the major college hockey mark for most shots turned away in a regulation game victory. Providence College's Ed Hornstein and RPI's Don Cutts also accomplished the feat. After Guimond's block party, RIT Coach Wayne Wilson offered his opinion.

> The sheer volume of shots was impressive. He gave everyone on the bench a real comfort level. It was one of those nights where the puck must have looked like a beach ball to him.

Interestingly, St. Lawrence pelted him again the next night, and although he stopped 37 shots, he also allowed six goals in a 6–3 loss.

"He obviously was a little fatigued, and who could blame him?" Wilson said. "He had nothing to be ashamed of. He turned away 103 shots. Some goaltenders don't turn away that many shots in 10 games, let alone two in two nights."

In other words, the goalie had a pretty good week or two that weekend.

Davis played her way into the RIT hockey record books by turning away 66 shots in a December 10, 1982 game against Clarkson University, while Ali Binnington made 62 saves in a double-overtime win against Mercyhurst University in the College Hockey America championship game on March 8, 2014. Binnington finished the season with a school-record 788 saves that season to earn CHA Goaltender of the Year honors—an honor she would repeat the following season.

Ali Binnington

The next night, RIT pummeled Augsburg (Minnesota) College, 10–1, in the consolation game to finish their season with a 29–6 record. Not long after the Union defeat, the Tigers suffered another loss when Mason left to take the Dartmouth College head coaching job. When he was hired at RIT, Mason said his goal was to coach at the Division I level some day and that he had hoped the Tigers program might make a decision to go that route. But that decision was still two decades away.

RIT
RIT
RIT
RIT

4.

A SECOND TITLE IN THREE YEARS

RIT Athletic Director Lou Spiotti wasn't lacking for coaching applicants following Brian Mason's departure after the 1983–84 season. With a national championship and two Final Four appearances in two years, the Tigers were on a roll, and the position had become one of most desirable in all of college hockey—a true plum job. From a pool of more than 50 candidates, Spiotti chose Bruce Delventhal to become the fifth coach in the program's 27-year history. It seemed a perfect fit, given Delventhal's background.

A native of Englewood, New Jersey, who grew up in the shadow of the George Washington Bridge, Delventhal played two seasons as a defenseman at Hamilton College under legendary American hockey coach Greg Batt. After graduating, he attended the Princeton divinity school, where he received his master's degree in 1975. While in graduate school, Delventhal served as a counselor at Calgary Hospital in the Bronx, working with terminally ill patients. Though that was a rewarding experience, Delventhal began missing hockey and aspired to become involved in the game again.

"Coaching is basically counseling and teaching," he said. "The thing I love about it is that you are not only teaching the Xs and Os of hockey, but also the Xs and Os of life. You really get involved in your players' lives. I believe that classrooms come in all different forms. Mine just happened to have a floor made of ice."

Like Mason, Delventhal wound up cutting his coaching teeth at Northwood Prep School in Lake Placid, where he posted an impressive 67–20–2 record in four seasons. His 1978 team went 25–4 and was ranked no. 1 nationally among prep schools by *Hockey Magazine*. From there, Delventhal landed a job at Princeton University, where he worked as a full-time assistant and primary recruiter for three seasons.

Delventhal was just 34 when he started at RIT. He realized immediately that he was walking into a potentially great situation, because Mason had left the cupboard so full you could barely close the door. Delventhal inherited a roster with 18 returning veteran players, including All-American center Chris Johnstone, high-scoring wings Bobby Trowell and Ritchie Herbert, and stout defensemen B.J. Hull, Blaise MacDonald and John Hawkins. The biggest question would be who would fill the void left

Opposite: The Tigers celebrate on ice, moments after winning the 1985 NCAA Division III title.

RIT went 26-6-1 during their 1984-85 championship season.

by All-American goaltender Dave Burkholder. Delventhal was confident that newcomers Chet Hallice and Rob Rohlfs would be up to the task of following Burkholder.

The abundance of talent coupled with RIT's recent success made for high expectations, and a great deal of pressure on the new head coach. Delventhal's new system and more forceful personality took some getting used to. Johnstone noted that the transition wasn't easy.

> It was difficult at first. There was some resistance on the part of the veterans. We were comfortable with Brian and sorry to see him go and we were a little skeptical of Bruce at first.

After a few weeks of head-butting, Johnstone, a tri-captain, called a players-only meeting. He told his teammates: "We can't keep living in the past." Then, he met privately with Delventhal and told him: "Don't panic. Some of us are having some problems with the transition, but that's normal. The main thing is we believe in what you're doing."

By the season opener they all were on the same page, and the Tigers got off on the right skate with a 2–1 victory over defending national champion Babson College. They dropped a 4–2 decision in the second game to Canadian powerhouse Wilfrid Laurier before going on a roll. But despite an 18–4–1 start that saw RIT in the thick of national championship contention, skeptics remained. The shadow of Mason loomed large on campus. To illustrate this, Delventhal related an encounter with a professor following an 8–5 come-from-behind win against Geneseo in February.

"Some game last night," the professor said.

Captains Blaise MacDonald, Gump Whiteside and Chris Johnstone pictured with Coach Bruce Delventhal (third from left).

"Well, we like to keep things interesting," joked Delventhal, whose team had overcome a two-goal deficit heading into the final period.

"I just hope we have them ready for the playoffs," said the professor, leaving the room before Delventhal could respond.

Not long after that encounter, the coach spoke his mind to a reporter.

> It's a double-edged sword when you come into a winning situation. People are used to success and they want to see it continue. That's understandable. What frustrates me is that we have carried the torch and kept things going in the right direction here, but you still find some people who aren't pleased. Fortunately, it's just a few people who don't understand. It's not a lot.

At that point, Delventhal realized that anything short of a national championship would be considered a disappointment by his critics. "In a way, that didn't bother me because I felt we had the type of team that was capable of giving it a good shot at winning it all," he said.

On the basis of their 21–5–1 record (which included a loss and a tie to Division I schools, along with a defeat against a Canadian team), the Tigers earned the right to host the ECAC West Region Division II tournament at Ritter Arena. After defeating Oswego in the opener, RIT met Union College in a much-anticipated rematch of their semifinal game the year before that saw the Dutchmen win in four overtimes. Goalie Wayne McDougall had shut down the Tigers in that game, making 61 saves. And he was hot again in the rematch, turning away 50 shots as Union defeated them, 7–3. The loss cost RIT the top seed and the opportunity to host the Final Four for a second straight season.

Captains of the 1984-85 championship team: Gump Whiteside, Blaise MacDonald and Chris Johnstone.

The Tigers did earn the right to host the College of St. Thomas from St. Paul, Minnesota, in a two-game, total goal series for the right to advance to NCAA semifinals. RIT won the first game, 5–4, on Chris Johnstone's goal. The Tommies went up 2–1 in the second game, meaning the two-game score was tied. Rohlfs had struggled in net during the first period, prompting Delventhal to switch back to Hallice in the second period. The move worked out marvelously as Hallice blanked St. Thomas the rest of the way and RIT came back to record a 5–2 victory and its third consecutive berth in the Final Four.

This time the road to the championship would go through Union College, which had earned the right to host the semifinals and finals at Achilles Rink in Schenectady, New York. Several veteran players from the 1982–83 national title team couldn't help but see similarities between this trip and the journey they'd taken two years earlier when they had to beat top-ranked Lowell on its home ice. But Johnstone saw one major difference.

> This definitely is a better team than the team that won it all. We were probably the fourth best team there (in 1983). It was just our weekend.

As had been the case then, they would rely on the torrid play of a goaltender all the way to a national championship.

Hallice had alternated in goal with Rohlfs for much of the season, and although he had played well, he often incurred his coach's wrath.

"There were about a half a dozen guys I rode pretty good that season and he was one of them," Delventhal recalled. "They'd actually put up odds in the locker room for who I'd yell at the most. Blaise (MacDonald)

Bobby Trowell scores his second goal in a 3-2 victory vs. Lowell in the 1985 NCAA semifinals.

joked that Chet was going off at 2–1."

Though only a freshman, Hallice proved to have skin as thick as shin guards. After watching him kick shot after shot away in warm-ups, Delventhal told him he would be starting against Union in the semifinals. Hallice, who played at Northwood Prep and first caught Delventhal's eye when he was recruiting as a Princeton assistant, wasn't too surprised.

"I had an idea I might start. But I'm glad he didn't tell me until after warm-ups. If I had known a couple of days beforehand, I would have been a wreck."

The start of the RIT–Union game on March 22, 1985 was delayed nearly an hour because it took Bemidji three overtimes to defeat Plattsburgh State in the other semifinal round.

"The delay actually helped." Delventhal said. "We sat around in the locker room telling jokes that aren't fit for print. Me included."

The coach couldn't believe how calm he felt.

"I'm usually pretty uptight before a game. Usually I try to leave the team alone. But I was the loosest guy."

McDougall deflected a slap shot from the blue line by Bobby Trowell a little more than 12 minutes into the game. But Trowell skated quickly to the puck and flicked it over the goalie's glove and into the net to put RIT up 1–0. The Tigers went up by two goals 12 seconds into the second period when Johnstone took the opening face-off, bore in on the net and beat McDougall with a low, hard shot into the left-hand corner of the net. The goal—his 114th—made Johnstone RIT's all-time leading scorer, a distinction he still holds.

It appeared the Tigers were in complete control, but Union sliced the deficit to one just 35 seconds later on Todd Hodgin's goal. A few minutes later, the Dutchmen tied the game when Jamie Knight smacked a rebound past Hallice.

Trowell's second goal came on a power play with six minutes and 33 seconds remaining in the second period. McDougall had kicked away a slap shot by Jeff Mercier, but Trowell was there to stuff the rebound into the net for a 3–2 lead. That goal proved to be the difference as Hallice stopped 17 shots to preserve a 3–2 victory. The game was sweet vindication for the Tigers after the previous season's marathon loss to Union and the four-goal loss in the 1985 ECACs—both on RIT ice. "That felt like the championship game to us," Trowell said.

Delventhal ordered pizzas delivered to the team hotel. As the players wolfed down their slices, defenseman John Hawkins reminded his teammates that their assignment was only half complete. Bemidji, whom they had beaten two years earlier for the Division II title, was the only team standing in the way of another national crown.

Hallice and some of his teammates whiled away the time the next day playing cards in the hotel. Trowell went shopping and bought a pair of sunglasses and four victory cigars. At 2:30, the team ate a spaghetti dinner. Trowell kept repeating the slogan "Make it happen" to anyone within earshot. At 4 o'clock, Blaise MacDonald went to church with some teammates and said a few extra prayers.

Perhaps there was a bit of a letdown, or perhaps they were just spent from all the energy they'd poured

NO DOUBTING THIS THOMAS

The news that Artie Thomas had been diagnosed with Hodgkin's lymphoma in December 1994 hit his coach and RIT hockey teammates harder than a cross-check to the head.

"You don't expect to hear that kind of a diagnosis with a seemingly, strong, healthy young man," Tigers coach Eric Hoffberg recalled. "It knocks you for a loop. But I knew Artie was given a good chance to survive and I knew he was a fighter. I believed he would battle back."

Thomas was determined to skate for the Tigers again. Not only did the forward skate again, he excelled. After weeks of painful, at times debilitating, chemotherapy and radiation treatments, Thomas was able to resume workouts. By the following season, he was back on the ice, tallying 38 points in 32 games during his comeback campaign. The next season—1996–97—he was named captain and finished fifth in scoring with 31 points on 15 goals and 16 assists.

Artie Thomas

After completing his career, Thomas continued to give back to his alma mater as a student recruiter and assistant hockey coach. Thanks to Hoffberg, his legacy with the program continues. Each year, since 1998, the Art Thomas Teammate Award has been presented to a player who embodies the tenacity and selflessness of the former RIT standout who successfully battled back from cancer.

into the previous night's victory against Union, but for some reason the Tigers seemed lackluster during the scoreless first period of the championship game. Hallice, in goal for his fourth consecutive game, took it as a good omen. "I knew after that period that we'd win," he said. "It was 0–0 and it wasn't our best period of hockey." MacDonald called it a "horrible period." Delventhal concurred. In hopes of shaking them from their lethargy, he lit into them during the first intermission. "I scolded them a bit," he said. "I said, 'Let's wake up and play hockey.'"

The alarm must have gone off in the second period, because Pete Schroeder and Ritchie Herbert scored to give RIT a 2–0 lead heading into the final period. Before heading out for the final 20 minutes of play, Delventhal warned his team to remain aggressive. "Don't go into a shell," he told them. "Keep forcing it. Play like you're down two."

Trowell pounced on a loose puck in front of the Union goal and flung it into the net to make it 3–0 less than three minutes after the final period began. Todd Lescarbeau finally got Bemidji on the board 85 seconds later, but that would be the Beavers' last gasp. Late in the game, they pulled their goalie so they could skate a sixth attacker. The desperation strategy backfired as Larry Shomphe slid the puck down the ice and into the empty net to put RIT up 4–1 with a minute and 15 seconds remaining. Trowell closed out the scoring with another goal with seven seconds to go as the Tigers won their second national championship in three years.

When the horn sounded, the RIT players celebrated by piling on one another near one of the goals. "I'm so

Chet Hallice's torrid goaltending played a pivotal role in the Tigers winning their second championship in three seasons.

RIT
HULL
5

NCAA

excited," yelled Blaise MacDonald, "that I've got goose bumps on my fingernails!" For Hallice and Delventhal, there was a sense not only of joy, but also of relief. Each had to deal with the enormous pressure of succeeding a legend. They had answered the call, made believers of skeptics. "It's the luck of the Irish," said Hallice, who wore a shamrock on the back of his goalie's mask. He had never heard of RIT until it won the NCAA title two years earlier. He knew of the program now, and had helped author a new chapter in its history by making 44 saves in the Final Four to win tournament MVP honors. "I thought about what this might feel like," he said. "I knew it would be a great feeling, but I never expected anything like this." He said his defensemen were as much a part of this award as he was. Indeed, MacDonald, Russ Firman, John Hawkins, Mike Jones, Tom Herstad and Maurice Montambault had done a superb job of holding Bemidji's scorers in check and clearing rebounds.

With seven goals in his final three games, Trowell could also have been named MVP.

"Can you believe that Bobby Trowell?" MacDonald said. " That goal has been like a magnet for him the past couple of games. He just fires the puck and it heads into the goal automatically."

In the locker room, the players doused Delventhal with champagne. "I guess," he told a reporter, "we won't have to answer any questions about how good we are any more." MacDonald, who would earn

Opposite: The Tigers celebrate their 4-1 victory against Bemidji in the 1985 title game.

Right: Defenseman Blaise MacDonald leaps into a teammate's arms after the final buzzer.

FOR WHOM THE BELL TOLLS

Steve Toll excelled in two sports.

You can make a strong case that no player in RIT's illustrious hockey history had a season as dominating as the one Steve Toll had in 1996–97. In fact, that winter he was the Tigers' version of Wayne Gretzky. A native of St. Catharines, Ontario, Canada, Toll established school records for goals (39) and points (84) in a season, averaging more than a goal (1.3) and nearly three points (2.8) per game as RIT went 21–7–3. During a four-game stretch from October 19 through November 8, 1996, he tallied a school-record four consecutive hat tricks (three-goal games). Toll finished with six hat tricks, which also is a school mark. His dominance did not go unnoticed, as the American Hockey Coaches Association named him national player of the year.

Following that historic season, Toll signed a professional contract with the Raleigh Ice Caps of the East Coast Hockey League and recorded a goal and three assists in seven games. The following year, he took the Central Hockey League by storm by combining for 25 goals and 41 assists in 66 games while splitting time between the Fayetteville Force and the Columbus Cottonmouths. "After I tore it up at RIT, and early into my ECHL career, I thought I had a legitimate shot (at making the National Hockey League)," he said in a 2007 interview with Laxmag.com. "Things didn't work out, but it was fun."

The travel—which included 24-hour-long bus trips—eventually took its toll on Toll, and he retired from professional hockey after just four seasons. But he didn't retire from sports. In fact, Toll would go on to make an even bigger mark as a lacrosse player and establish himself as the most successful professional athlete RIT has ever produced. In 14 seasons in the National Lacrosse League, the player known as "Speedin' Stevie" because of his blazing speed scored 170 goals and 452 points in 219 games. Along the way, he was part of five NLL championships—four with the Toronto Rock and one with the Rochester Knighthawks. In 2007, he was named the league's top transition specialist.

Tigers players show off their championship rings.

RIT Coach Bruce Delventhal hoists the 1985 NCAA championship trophy in a ceremony before a Rochester Americans game at the War Memorial.

All-American honors as a defenseman that year, praised the rookie head coach. "He came into a pressure-packed situation and immediately grabbed control of the players. He got us to believe in his system, and more importantly, believe in him."

As had been the case two years earlier, there was another pep rally on campus to celebrate the Tigers' lofty achievement. On the rollicking four-hour bus ride home from Schenectady that Sunday, Hallice clutched the MVP trophy the entire way. "You would have thought he was holding onto his firstborn," MacDonald joked. Delventhal sat in his customary seat up front. One by one, players stopped by to thank him.

"That's why I coach," Delventhal said. "I like people. You know when somebody you love a lot does something good? That's how I felt."

MARTIN
14
27
28
19
BAUER
EASTON

5.

A MAGICAL TRIP TO THE FROZEN FOUR

He had spent the first 16 years of his life in hockey-mad Montreal, dreaming about becoming the next Bobby Orr. Like his legendary Boston Bruins idol, Wayne Wilson played defense, and though he was good enough to captain Bowling Green University to an NCAA Division I championship in 1984, he wasn't quite good enough to make a go of it professionally. A heady player whom some regarded as a coach on the ice, Wilson wanted in the worst way to stay involved in the game, so when legendary Bowling Green coach Jerry York asked him to help out as a graduate assistant coach, Wilson jumped at the offer. And that's what he did, when he wasn't attending classes while working toward a master's degree in recreational facility management, which he received in 1986.

"It was a great experience," Wilson recalled of his time as a part-time coach. "It kept me in the game I loved, and I got to learn the finer points of coaching from one of the legendary teachers of the game."

After receiving his master's, Wilson took a full-time assistant's job with the University of New Hampshire hockey program, but the following year York had a full-time opening and invited his former player and coach back to Bowling Green. Wilson would remain at his alma mater for the next 11 seasons.

> I loved it, and like most assistants I had a dream of becoming a head coach someday. I wanted to take what I had learned from Jerry and others and apply that knowledge to running my own team.

About six years into the stint at Bowling Green, Wilson began applying for some head coaching openings. He interviewed at Niagara University, but lost out to former RIT All-American Blaise MacDonald. He also interviewed at Union College after former Tigers head coach Bruce Delventhal left the Dutchmen program, but again failed to land the job. When the RIT position opened in 1999, Wilson interviewed once more. The third time proved to be a charm. Tigers athletics director Lou Spiotti and the search committee were thoroughly impressed and hired Wilson to replace Eric Hoffberg. Spiotti recalled those pre-hiring talks with Wilson.

Opposite: A flurry in front of the net during the NCAA East Regionals between RIT and Denver.

> He was eminently qualified. His hockey pedigree as a player and coach was outstanding, and we could tell immediately in the interviews that he would relate well with our student athletes. We had a great vibe about him the instant we met him. We felt Wayne would be a perfect fit.

It also helped that Wilson had a master's in facility management, because part of his job involved managing the rink at Ritter Arena.

Wilson was quite familiar with RIT's reputation for hockey excellence. He had worked numerous camps with Delventhal. And another former Tigers head coach, Buddy Powers, had spent several years with Wilson on the Bowling Green staff. He also knew that Scott Brown, a former Tigers All-American, hailed from his Canadian hometown, Guelph.

"Everybody I knew sang RIT's praises; it was a well-respected, small-college hockey program," Wilson said. " I didn't want to just take a position to say, 'Hey, I'm a head coach.' I was thinking, 'Hey, if I do a really good job here, this might be a springboard to a Division I program,' and if not, I wanted to make sure I was in a situation where this could be a job I could have for the rest of my life."

Little did he know at the time, but the RIT job would become one he might have for the rest of his career and one that also would become a springboard to Division I.

"When I first got the job, I remember reporters asking me at the press conference if we were going to go Division I," he said. "I had never heard the question before and it kind of caught me by surprise. I told them, 'Not that I know of.' I'm sure some people in the media thought I was being coy, because, unbeknownst to

Wayne Wilson

me, the rumors of RIT going DI had been percolating for years. But I was being honest. It really never had come up during my interviews for the job. And it wouldn't become an issue until a few years later."

The adjustment from a major-college hockey program to a small-college hockey program was not an easy one for Wilson. The workload increased dramatically. He was forced to become a jack-of-all-trades, which was a challenge.

> At Bowling Green, we had a head coach, two full-time assistants and a grad assistant—and we had a decent budget for recruiting, etc. At RIT, I had a great assistant in Art Thomas, but he wasn't full-time. He actually worked in admissions, so he couldn't join us until we were about halfway through practice each day. And he was on the road until November, recruiting students—not hockey players, but regular students—for RIT, so, in essence I really didn't have his part-time services until the season was about to start. In addition to coaching, I

> was the equipment manager and the rink manager. I spent any time I could find on weekends or week nights getting into my car and driving to places to check out recruits. One year, I decided to log all the time I put in and it came out to about 80 hours per week. But that's how it is when you are a Division III coach. People in Division I have no idea just how hard these guys work.

Despite the crazy schedule, Wilson managed just fine.

> I give a lot of credit to the captains and upperclassmen we had. You need good leaders among your players because, in a way, they become like assistant coaches for you. I was very fortunate. I had several captains who were very mature and very committed to helping out.

Forward Pat Staerker, a 2000 RIT graduate, was a three-time All-American.

Led by senior captain Pat Staerker, who became the first RIT player to garner All-American honors in three consecutive seasons, Wilson's first Tigers team went 21–7–1 and reached the NCAA quarterfinals, where it lost to Norwich. Wilson's second season proved to be one of the best in school history as RIT posted a 27–1–1 record, reaching the NCAA championship game, which it lost to Plattsburgh, 6–2, on home ice at Ritter. Four players—Peter Bournazakis, Tyler Euverman, Jerry Galway and Derek Hahn—were named first-team All-Americans, and Wilson was voted the American Hockey Coaches Association Coach of the Year. "It was just an unbelievable season," Wilson said. "But I guess the fairy tale didn't end the way we wanted it to."

The Tigers compiled another excellent record during the 2001–02 season, going 23–2–2, but again came up short in the NCAA tournament, losing a quarterfinal series to Plattsburgh, that required a mini-game to determine who advanced. After a 20–6–2 mark the following season, the Tigers experienced mediocre campaigns in 2003–04 and 2004–05, going 13–7–5 and 15–11–1, respectively.

But the big news during that time involved a long-time rumor that was about to come true. After decades of discussion on campus and in the community, RIT President Al Simone made the decision to go Division I in hockey. Because the school was joining the NCAA's highest division in one sport only, RIT would not be allowed to give out athletic scholarships. This would put the Tigers at a distinct competitive disadvantage because the overwhelming majority of schools it would play against would field scholarship players. But Simone and Spiotti believed RIT could still succeed. Wilson had some ideas about how to go about it.

RIT President Al Simone (left) and athletic director Lou Spiotti (right) at the 2004 press conference announcing the decision to elevate the men's hockey program from Division III to Division I.

> I knew it was going to be a huge challenge, especially convincing kids to come to RIT without an athletic scholarship. But you just have to be creative. We sell the academic excellence of our school and the unique programs we have to offer. We definitely go after students interested in becoming engineers. I remember people wondering how we got a kid like Sean Murphy from Minnesota to come here, instead of going to one of the hockey powers in the Midwest. Well, he wanted a strong engineering program, and he knew we had one of the best. We've had a season where we had four pre-med students on our roster. We know we aren't necessarily going to get the blue-chippers, the kids that are going to be drafted by National Hockey League teams. But we can get kids who might have slipped through the cracks, kids who have something to prove, kids who like being part of an underdog program.

One of RIT's first priorities would be finding a suitable Division I conference to join. Spiotti realized that trying to make a go of it as an independent would be next to impossible because most schools would then refuse to schedule away games with the Tigers, meaning they would be forced to play virtually every game on the road. RIT's timing proved impeccable because the Atlantic Hockey Association had an immediate opening after another school decided to drop its men's hockey program. Spiotti was relieved.

> That was a godsend for us. That solved so many of our scheduling issues. Plus, we were joining a conference featuring schools that share our academic mission.

The AHA, which boasted schools such as the U.S. Military Academy, the Air Force Academy, American International and Quinnipiac, welcomed RIT into the fold in time for the 2005–06 season, the only caveat being that the Tigers would not be eligible for the conference's post-season tournament until their third year.

Wilson approached that first season in DI with equal parts excitement and trepidation.

> I had been removed from that level for so long that I didn't know how we'd match up with the speed and strength of those top-of-the-line players. I thought I had some pretty good players, but there's a huge difference between DIII players and guys who might be a year or two or three away from playing in the NHL. So, yeah, I was concerned. I didn't want us to embarrass ourselves.

RIT won the Atlantic Hockey Association regular-season title in 2007 in only its second season in Division I.

Although the Tigers went just 9–24–2, they acquitted themselves quite well. On October 15, 2005, they made history, beating Air Force, 5–2, for their first victory as a DI program. Wilson felt good about the season.

> In retrospect, that's probably one of the most rewarding years I've had here. Yeah, we had a losing record, but the thing that impressed me most was that our guys came to compete, every single time they took the ice, even though they were overmatched skill-wise and size-wise and speed-wise in every game. It would have been easy for them to throw in the towel. That was probably the most competitive team I've ever coached. Not my best team. But my most competitive. I really admired those kids.

The Tigers proved they could indeed compete at that level. Bolstered by a solid recruiting class and the return of several hungry veterans out to show that they had been overlooked by the big-time programs, RIT went 21–11–2 in its second season as a DI program and won the AHA regular-season title.

"That was a big boost for us," Wilson said. "That gave us confidence that we weren't overmatched, that we could not only play at this level, but have some success because the big thing is not just to go DI just to say you are DI, but to be good at it."

In 2007–08, the Tigers posted a 19–12–6 mark and appeared primed to win the AHA tournament and earn their first Division I NCAA berth. But after scoring two overtime wins against Holy Cross, RIT was trounced, 5–0, by Air Force, in front of a large but disappointed crowd at the Blue Cross Arena in downtown Rochester. The next season, the Tigers improved to 23–13–2, but suffered the same disappointment in the post-season, this time losing to Mercyhurst, 5–4, in overtime—again in the AHA semifinals, again on home ice. "It was terribly disappointing," Wilson said. "There was a hump we definitely needed to get over."

Wilson was brimming with optimism heading into the 2009–10 season—with good reason. He had 19 players returning—including senior captains Dan Ringwald and Stevan Matic and junior assistant captains Sean Murphy and Andrew Favot—plus six highly touted newcomers, including defenseman Chris Tanev, who would become the first player from RIT to play in the National Hockey League.

> I thought we might be on the verge of a breakthrough season. I really liked our team. I could just feel it in my gut. We had a lot of talented guys returning and we had brought in a good group of recruits and they all seemed to mesh. Coaches can usually tell early on what they have and whether the team chemistry is going to be good or bad, and whether the pieces are going to fit together. I had a belief that this team had an opportunity to be really good.

And Wilson continued to believe, despite a disappointing start that saw the Tigers open with a 3–2 victory against York University, then drop five games in a row. They followed that streak with eight consecutive wins, but after a tie and another victory, they dropped three

SIMON SAYS: I CAN PLAY AT THIS LEVEL

Simon Lambert clearly saved his best for last. During his senior season in 2007–08, he finished first in the American Hockey Association and sixth in the nation in scoring with 21 goals, 30 assists and 51 points. Writers and broadcasters were so impressed with the season the center had for the 19–12–6 Tigers that they voted him a finalist for the Hobey Baker Award, which is presented annually to the nation's top player. He is the only player in RIT history to be a finalist for college hockey's version of the Heisman Trophy.

What makes Lambert's accomplishment even more impressive is that he wasn't recruited by any Division I program. Coach Wayne Wilson was able to convince the Quebec native to attend RIT in 2004–05, when the Tigers were still playing at the Division III level. "I was able to dangle the carrot that we would be going Division I the next season," Wilson recalled. "So he knew he'd be getting the opportunity to play at a level that most coaches didn't think he could play at."

As a sophomore, Lambert proved he was more than ready to compete at the highest level of college hockey as he helped the Tigers make the transition from Division III. Although they finished with a 9–24–2 record, they were within striking distance in the majority of their games. "They pulled their goalie 21 times, meaning they were close enough to have a chance to win at the end," said longtime RIT broadcaster and national hockey writer Chris Lerch. "And it was guys like Simon who gave them the opportunities to be in that position of holding their own." Lambert finished his career as the school's all-time goal scorer in Division I with 55. "He definitely was one of those talents who slipped through the cracks," Lerch said. "Here's a guy who went from being a Division III player to one of the top players in all of college hockey. Pretty amazing."

more games and found themselves stuck with a mediocre 10–8–1 record midway through the season. He was confident things would turn around.

> We were a little streaky at the start, but I saw no reason to panic, because I saw the talent that we had. I figured if we weathered the storm, we could make hay against our league opponents from that point on and we could have a nice finishing kick.

Which is what happened, as the Tigers won 13 of their next 16 games to win their third Atlantic Hockey Association regular season title in four years. Once again, they would host the conference's post-season tournament at the Blue Cross Arena, and this time they would finish the job, by sweeping Connecticut, 4–3 and 4–1, in the quarterfinal series, before disposing of Canisius, 4–0, in the semifinals and Sacred Heart, 6–1, in the title game to earn a spot in the NCAA tournament. Jared DeMichiel, a scarcely recruited goalie from Avon, Connecticut, continued his torrid play, turning away one shot after another. He set the tone in the semifinal victory when he stopped a point-blank shot by Canisius forward Scott Moser on a breakaway just 28 seconds into the game. That would be about as close as the Golden Griffins would come to scoring that night as DeMichiel made 20 saves. "I told myself before the game my team is going to play great in front of me and maybe I need to make a couple of good saves," he said. "One of them came earlier than expected." The following night, in front of 3,298 noisy, mostly orange-clad RIT fans, the Tigers routed Sacred Heart as tournament most valuable player Cameron Burt scored a goal and assisted on four others, including two by Sean Murphy. Afterward, Wilson spoke to reporters about the team's status.

Goalie Jared DeMichiel fueled RIT's Frozen Four run.

The Tigers celebrate their first Atlantic Hockey Association tournament title in 2010.

> The last couple of years really taught us lessons. We learned from the past and we applied (those lessons) to now and we've set another standard for Division I hockey for RIT. It's always been our goal to get into the NCAAs and take it game-by-game from there.

Although the Tigers had won 10 straight, they headed to the NCAA East regionals at the Albany Times–Union Center as heavy underdogs. The committee had seeded them 15th in the 16-team tournament field, meaning they would be facing No. 2 seed Denver, which had been ranked at or near the top of the college hockey polls throughout the season. Fourteen players on the Denver roster had been drafted by National Hockey League teams, including goalie Marc Cheverie, who had a 24–5–3 record and was a finalist for the Hobey Baker Award, which was presented annually to the top collegiate player. That was 14 more draft picks than the RIT roster boasted. Despite the odds, Wilson was confident his team would be competitive against the favored Pioneers from the Western Collegiate Hockey Association, one of the nation's power conferences. "We're not looking at this as David vs. Goliath," he said. And neither was Denver coach George Gwozdecky, who told reporters: "Everybody who follows college hockey—fans, coaches, players—understands that at this point, every team is good, every team is competitive and there is no easy game." Hockey insiders appeared to agree, one of them noting that Denver, despite its lofty reputation, had not won a national championship since 2005, their second of back-to-back titles.

One of the main reasons Wilson felt good about his team's chances was the play of DeMichiel. A hot

Players and fans celebrate at the Blue Cross Arena after RIT defeats Sacred Heart, 6-1, in the 2010 AHA title game.

RIT IN THE NHL

On May 31, 2010—just seven weeks after RIT's riveting run to the NCAA Frozen Four—Chris Tanev signed a contract with the Vancouver Canucks of the National Hockey League, forgoing his final three years of college hockey eligibility. The decision caught Tigers coach Wayne Wilson by surprise. Although he had been thoroughly impressed with his freshman defenseman, who had earned Atlantic Hockey Association Rookie of the Year honors following a season in which he recorded 10 goals and 28 points in 41 games, Wilson believed Tanev would benefit from another season or two at the college level.

> I didn't think he was ready. Shows you what I know. A year after playing for us in the Frozen Four, he's playing defense in Game Seven of the Stanley Cup Finals.

Tanev holds the distinction of being the first RIT alumnus to play a game in the NHL, making his debut on January 18, 2011. Six days later, he scored his first point when he assisted on a teammate's power-play goal. A native of the Toronto suburb of East York, Ontario, Tanev became the first RIT player to score an NHL goal when he fired the puck into the net in an overtime victory over the Edmonton Oilers on February 4, 2013.

Tanev is far from being the first RIT player to sign a professional hockey contract. That honor belongs to Chris Palmer, who inked a deal with the New Jersey Devils organization in 1990 after a three-year career that saw him score 174 points for the Tigers. Several others would follow Palmer's lead, including Steve Pinizzotto, who left

Chris Tanev

Chris Palmer

school early to sign with the Washington Capitals on March 19, 2007. Two years later, Pinizzotto was called up to the big club. Although he skated in warm-ups, he did not dress, and was sent back down to the Capitals' minor-league affiliate in Hershey, Pennsylvania the next day. He wound up making his NHL debut in 2013 and was a teammate of Tanev's for 12 games that season.

On June 26, 2015, former RIT women's hockey captain Celeste Brown became the first player in program history to sign a professional contract, inking a deal with the New York Riveters of the newly formed National Women's Hockey League. She is the school's all-time Division I scoring leader with 30 goals.

A number of RIT alumni, including 2008 Hobey Baker finalist Simon Lambert, opted to play for pay in Europe. No one is happier than Wilson about the increasing opportunities for former Tigers to turn pro once their collegiate careers are through. "It's exciting to see the spike in interest among NHL teams in our program," he said. "To tell a kid that you can come to a place like RIT and get a world-class education and still have an opportunity to pursue the dream of playing professional hockey is just another thing we can hang our hat on."

RIT's 2009-10 team went 28-12-1 during its Frozen Four season.

goaltender can carry a team, and DeMichiel clearly had been doing just that. In fact, his stats, which included a nation-leading 25 victories and a 2.00 goals-against average, were superior to those compiled by Cheverie. DeMichiel had emerged as a team leader on and off the ice—this despite the fact that even his teammates had difficulty pronouncing and spelling his name. (For the record, it's pronounced Dee-Michelle, and was misspelled the first few times he made the dean's list.)

"He probably should be wearing a C for "captain" on his jersey," Wilson said. "He is not afraid to speak up. And he knows how to keep us loose. He has a great, strong work ethic. He is invaluable right now."

After DeMichiel's performance in a 2–1 upset of Denver in the first NCAA Division I tournament game in school history, some believed he should have had an S for "Superman" on his jersey. The Pioneers outshot the Tigers by a wide margin, 40–24, but DeMichiel turned away 39 of the pucks fired his way. Defenseman Chris Tanev scored an unassisted goal five minutes into the game, and Cameron Burt converted a pass from Dan Ringwald on a power play with 7:24 remaining in the third period to give RIT a 2–0 advantage. Denver finally scored with 5:26 left in the game as Joe Colborne tucked in a pass from Tyler Ruegsegger on a power play, but that would be the only time the Pioneers got one past DeMichiel. In the post-game interviews, everyone was raving about RIT's netminder. "It's tough when you're getting your chances and the goalie just keeps stopping you," Colborne said. Denver left wing Rhett Rakhshani

Chris Tanev was the Atlantic Hockey Association's 2009-10 rookie of the year.

Cameron Burt celebrates the game-winning goal vs. Denver in the 2010 NCAA East Regional semifinals.

concurred, saying, "Their goalie played great and they worked their butts off."

The victory occurred in front of what amounted to a home-away-from-home crowd for RIT. "We had our own fans who had made the trip down the Thruway," DeMichiel said. "But we also had fans in the building who were rooting for us because we were the underdogs." Wilson praised the support of the fans and the school's administration for helping the Tigers score the biggest victory in RIT history.

> School officials picked up half the ticket prices for the students, so that was a huge boost. I think we may have caught Denver taking us lightly. We had a pretty good goalie that got hot at the right time, and with it being on television, we had longer timeouts for the commercials, and that enabled us to play guys like Tanev a little longer. We weren't nearly as deep as Denver was, talent-wise, so being able to keep our top players out there a tad longer factored into our ability to go toe-to-toe with them.

The following night the magic continued as the Tigers breezed by the University of New Hampshire, 6–2, in front of a crowd of 3,737 at the Times-Union Center. RIT wrested control of the game away from UNH in the second period, outshooting them 18–6 and scoring three goals to take a commanding 4–1 lead. Right wing Tyler Brenner broke a 1–1 tie with the first of his two goals at

Opening faceoff between RIT (orange jerseys) and New Hampshire at the 2010 NCAA East Regional finals in Albany.

13:23 of the second period. Thirteen seconds later, before the announcement of Brenner's goal could be made over the P.A. system, Brent Alexin beat goalie Brian Foster. Then Stevan Matic gave RIT a three-goal lead at the 14:57 mark, and the game was essentially over.

DeMichiel was superb again, and was named the regional's most outstanding player following a two-game performance that saw him stop 63 of 66 shots. Forwards Brenner and Burt and defensemen Ringwald and Chris Haltigin joined the goalie on the All-Tourney team. The ramifications of the win were enormous. Just five years after making the quantum leap to Division I, RIT had turned the college hockey world on its ear, earning a berth in the Frozen Four, which would be played that year inside Ford Field, the home of the Detroit Lions of the National Football League.

ESPN.com's David Albright wrote admiringly of the team.

> RIT? How about RIP, for the remains from the carnage that has been created in the first two days of the 2010 NCAA Hockey Tournament? Quick, show of hands: Who had the Rochester Institute of Technology advancing to the Frozen Four? A better question might be: How many of you knew RIT played Division I hockey?

Wilson and his players were understandably ecstatic in the post-game press conferences. Many of them used the word "surreal" to describe the moment. "You kind of get lost in the excitement of what's happening," said junior center Andrew Favot, who set up the go-ahead goal against New Hampshire. "It's all a blur. I'm waiting to wake up." Burt, a Detroit native, was elated about the prospect of being able to play for a national title in his hometown. "The boys are all over me, saying I better have some connections and stuff for us to do when we get to the Motor City," he said. Ringwald echoed many of his teammates when he talked about how he was thrilled but not surprised by these victories. "I can tell you this: thirty guys in our dressing room definitely believed it could happen," he said. "We expected to win." The organizers of the regional tournament apparently had been caught by surprise. They had made up regional championship baseball caps with the school logos of the three other schools, in anticipation that they would be distributing them to Denver, New Hampshire or Cornell following Saturday's title game. Several years later, Wilson spoke of that night with a smile.

Tigers players salute the fans who made the trip to Albany for RIT's 6-2 victory against New Hampshire in the 2010 NCAA East Regional championship game.

> We were the only school they hadn't prepared victory hats for. Like many others, they didn't figure we had a snowball's chance in hell of winning it. That's okay. Just made the victories all the more sweeter.

On the bus ride home, Wilson checked his cell phone. He couldn't keep up with all the texts he had received from well-wishers. "I tried answering everybody, but it was impossible," he said. "I heard from relatives I didn't even know I had."

What had been hailed as the biggest collegiate sports victory in Rochester history touched off celebrations back in the Flower City that began that Saturday night and spilled into Sunday morning. Once the final horn sounded on the victory over New Hampshire, many of the nearly 120 RIT students, fans and alumni who had watched the game on large-screen televisions at T.C. Riley's Sports Pub near campus exchanged hugs and high-fives and began chanting: "Dee-Troit! Dee-Troit! Dee-Troit!" Justin Bissell, an applied mathematics major, was among the revelers, shouting:

> This is the Frozen Four! Five of us are driving (to Detroit). We'll find a hotel when we get there or sleep in my car if we have to.

Andrew Van Allen, a senior bio-technology major, was just as ecstatic. The *Democrat and Chronicle* quoted him as saying,

OF MICS AND MEN

The tradition of broadcasting RIT hockey games began in the fall of 1982, with Randy Bloechl providing play-by-play on the campus radio station, WITR-FM (89.7). Ed Trefzger started out producing the broadcasts before joining Bloechl in the booth as the host of the pre-game show and the color analyst in the mid-1990s. Chris Lerch, a long-time college hockey writer, was added as another analyst not long after that. Interestingly, even though all three men are 1984 RIT graduates, they didn't really know one another during their undergraduate days. Over time they became good friends, bound by a shared passion for RIT hockey. And in the process of describing the program's history, they became a part of it. Their long-time dedication to Tigers hockey was recognized in 2007 when they were presented the Dr. Al Simone Distinguished Service Award, named after the RIT president.

"We were very lucky to have those three individuals commit their time to our program," RIT men's hockey coach Wayne Wilson said at the time. "Remarkably, most of them did it for free. They took time away from their families to be a part of our hockey family. They wound playing a role in increasing the popularity of our program and fulfilling a need, especially when we were on the road, and people couldn't be there."

Road games could occasionally be as challenging for the broadcast team as they were for the players and coaches, especially when RIT was visiting longtime rivals like Elmira or Oswego. Lerch recalled those days with a chuckle.

> We'd walk into Elmira's old hockey barn, and they'd start booing us—and we were just the broadcasters. Then, during games they would throw things at us—food, coins, ice cubes—whatever they could get their hands on. It could get really nasty down there, especially if RIT was winning.

There was another time, Lerch said, when Bloechl almost got into a fight with an opposing official scorer, who

This is the greatest thing that's ever happened to RIT. I've never seen an atmosphere like this. It's the perfect scenario for everyone to come together and bond over RIT hockey and the school.

Several miles away, at Jeremiah's, the victory party was every bit as raucous. The tavern's three owners had played hockey at RIT and when the Tigers won, they served up platters of free chicken wings. After the bars closed, hundreds of people gathered on campus for an early morning, impromptu welcome home reception for the team. "It was really humbling," said leading scorer Cameron Burt, when asked what went through his and his teammates' minds when the bus pulled into the lot near Ritter at a little past 2 o'clock in the morning. "It was just a surreal experience, something I'll never forget." Added defenseman Alan Mazur:

We could hardly get off the bus because the fans were crowding around and wanting to just touch us. It didn't even feel real. You felt like a star, a huge star. I've never experienced anything like it.

kept yelling at the referee for missing calls.

Randy had grown tired of listening to this homer whining, so he says on the air, "I didn't know the official scorer was an extra referee here," and the guy turns around and challenges Randy to a fight. I wound up losing my temper, too. I said to the guy, "Oh, yeah. Why don't you come up here if you're man enough." Meanwhile, Ed (Trefzger) is engineering our broadcast, and he's warning us that we're still on the air and our listeners can hear everything that's going on. It was like a scene out of the wild, wild West. But that's the way it was for a long time. Those rivalries were intense.

After the 2008–09 season, Bloechl retired from doing play-by-play to spend more time with his young family, and Trefzger took over his duties, with Lerch providing color, along with Scott Biggar and Nick Phelan. In 2008, the school's nationally honored SportsZone television network, under the guidance of Mark Fragale began telecasting RIT home games on Rochester's Time Warner Cable affiliate, with Gene Battaglia and John DiTullio handling the announcing chores. During the women's team run to a Division III national championship in 2012, WITR also began broadcasting their games as Phelan, Fernando Ellis and Renee Radwan described the action.

RIT announcers Chris Lerch, Randy Bloechl, and Ed Trefzger.

ALL-AMERICANS

Here is a list of the male RIT hockey players who have earned All-American honors:

Dave Burkholder	1983–84
Chris Johnstone	1983–84, '84–85
B.J. Hull	1983–84
Blaise MacDonald	1984–85
John Hawkins	1985–86
Scott Brown	1988–89
Tim Cordick	1988–89
Chris Palmer	1989–90
Bill Gall	1990–91
Jay Murphy	1993–94
Chris Maybury	1994–95, '95–96
Adam French	1995–96
Steve Toll	1996–97
Jamie Morris	1996–97
Bryan Cossette	1996–97
Pat Staerker	1997–98, '98–99, '99–00
Jerry Galway	1998–99, '00–01, '01–02
Pete Bournazakis	2000–01
Tyler Euverman	2000–01
Derek Hahn	2000–01
Mike Bournazakis	2001–02
Mike Tarantino	2003–04
Dan Ringwald	2009–10
Shane Madolora	2010–11
Matt Garbowsky	2014-15

Sophomore wing Scott Knowles wound up being hoisted up by the crowd and was passed around as if he were body surfing and riding a wave. "I was just thankful," joked Wilson, "that they didn't drop him." Few enjoyed the festivities more than RIT president Bill Destler, an enthusiastic sort who did not lack for school spirit. Asked about the impact of reaching the Frozen Four, Destler didn't mince words.

> It meant everything to the RIT community. Usually, as I like to say, we're a bunch of geeks and artists, all running around ragged to get our work done, so school spirit can be a little hard to come by. But that achievement excited our community like nothing I can ever remember.

The excitement surrounding RIT's improbable achievement was conveyed by various media outlets. The headline on ESPN.com's college page that night blared: "Getting Technical." NCAA.com asked: "Who are these guys?" And the next morning's *Democrat and Chronicle* led its sports section with a big, bold-type headline reading: "They're Grrreat! Frozen Four-bound RIT is a real Tiger."

The Tigers' underdog role would continue into the Frozen Four, which featured three storied college hockey programs—Wisconsin, Boston College and Miami of Ohio. Three No. 1 seeds had made it to Detroit, and then there was RIT, which had begun the 16-team tournament as the second-to-last seed and continued to be referred to by many national media outlets as Rochester Tech. The Tigers players and coaches weren't bothered by such errors. They had come to embrace their David vs. Goliath role, and were a loose, fun bunch in the days leading up to their trip to the Motor City. As DeMichiel put it:

When you're tight, holding your stick, worried about what's going to happen next, you're not going to play to the best of your ability. If you're having fun and just letting things happen and letting your talent and ability take over, you're going to play at a high level."

DeMichiel clearly had been practicing what he had been preaching. No member of the team appeared more relaxed. And no Tiger had been playing better than the goalie who attracted scant interest from college recruiters following his junior hockey career.

"He gives us a lot of confidence as a team," Wilson said. "When you are not worried about your back end (of your defense) so much, you can be more aggressive on the other end. He has done that for us. We're very fortunate to have him."

RIT was riding a 12-game winning streak into the Frozen Four. During the post-season the players had taken to wearing gray T-shirts bearing the slogan "Fear the Streak." It had nothing to do with the fact they hadn't lost a game in more than six weeks and everything to do with the team's unified approach. In the animal world, tigers travel in packs known as "streaks," and look out for one another. Hence the slogan.

"I don't think we really know what we're doing right now," DeMichiel said, a few days after he and his teammates had won the East Regional. "I think it might take a month down the road, or maybe even years down the road to realize what we're doing right now. We're living for the moment, having fun and are just excited to play."

Although team rules prohibited the players from growing beards during the regular season, Wilson relented and allowed his players to follow the age-old hockey tradition of growing playoff beards once the post-season began. Two years earlier, he had allowed beards to be grown in the AHA tournament, but they had to be neatly trimmed, no hair on the neck. After the Tigers were smoked by Air Force, 5–0, in the conference

These t-shirts became popular among players and students as the Tigers streaked to the 2010 Frozen Four.

semifinals, he prohibited facial hair in the following year's league playoffs. It didn't change the results. The clean-shaven Tigers wound up losing, 5–4 in overtime in the 2008–09 conference semifinals, so when his players pestered him about post-season beards—with no restrictions—before the 2009–10 AHA playoffs, Wilson told them they could put away their razors.

"I don't think that's why we're 6–0 in the post-season, but . . ." DeMichiel said. "We were egging him on and egging him on. 'Coach, let us grow beards. Let us try it out.' We've come too far to shave now."

The campus was abuzz with excitement during the week leading up to the team's departure for Detroit. By this time, the players had become celebrities on campus, often being stopped on the way to classes to sign autographs and pose for pictures. But unlike big-time college sports factories where student athletes often are allowed to slack off during tournament time, RIT's hockey players were required to stay focused on their academics and keep their grades up. As it turned out, they managed their juggling act just fine, posting a cumulative 3.3 grade point average in the semester leading up to the Frozen Four. Perhaps no one juggled better than forward Mark Cornacchia, a second-year finance major who received an NCAA Elite-88 scholarship, given annually to the player in the Frozen Four with the highest GPA (3.85). Cornacchia credited RIT's faculty for part of the players' academic success.

> The professors are really helpful and accommodating. It helps us a lot because we are trying to pair athletics and academics. It's a delicate balance and we're student-athletes, student first. There are ample distractions if you want to be distracted, but if you concentrate on school, there is no reason why you can't achieve high marks and play at a high level.

The 2010 Frozen Four was played in Ford Field, the 80,000-seat stadium that is home to the NFL's Detroit Lions.

Another academic high achiever was senior captain Dan Ringwald, who earned his management degree in just three years and had eschewed offers to play professionally in the East Coast Hockey League, deciding instead to return to RIT to work toward a master's degree and play one more year collegiately. Defenseman Chris Haltigin, a second-year biomedical science major with a 3.72 GPA, was another RIT hockey player who defied the dumb jock stereotype.

"The guys on the hockey team are a pretty smart bunch," he said. "A lot of people don't know how hard we have to work to maintain our marks and do as well as we do on the ice. It's a lot of work and a lot of energy."

Few were more focused than Haltigin, who had been given the nickname "Brainiac" by DeMichiel.

"De-Mike gets on me a little bit about being a rocket scientist," he said. "I guess I'm the one on the team that studies the hardest, even though there's a lot of us that are pretty smart. But I got the label as the guy that's a bit of a bookworm, and the glasses don't help."

The RIT hockey program clearly had galvanized the campus. Even students who had never attended a hockey game were caught up in the emotion of the moment. Peter Briggs, a general manager at the Barnes & Noble at Park Point on campus, told a reporter he could barely keep up with the demand for apparel for Tigers fans. "I was not expecting this, whatsoever," said Emily England, a second-year computer science major. "The whole world is finding out who we are." Steve Dispenza, a fifth-year mechanical engineering student, concurred, telling the *Messenger-Post* newspaper, "A lot of people are now realizing RIT exists."

On April 5, a day before the team was to depart, hundreds of students attended an outdoor showing of the film *Miracle*, which depicted the underdog U.S. hockey team's stunning march to the Olympic gold medal at the 1980 Winter Games in Lake Placid. The next morning, nearly 3,000 people stuffed Ritter Arena for the RIT hockey team's sendoff rally. Each player was introduced to the crowd and walked on a red carpet from the locker room to the seating area at the north end of the rink, right in front of the raucous Corner Crew cheering section. President Bill Destler wore an RIT jersey over his dress shirt and tie. Monroe County Executive Maggie Brooks and Rochester Mayor Bob Duffy, an RIT alumnus, presented a plaque to Wayne Wilson, proclaiming it "RIT

RIT's famed student/alumni cheering section – the Corner Crew – made its presence felt at Ford Field.

Hockey Day." The coach then grabbed the mic and told the vocal, enthusiastic crowd that his team was going to bring back a national championship. Lou Spiotti, the long-time athletic director who had hired Wilson and spearheaded the move to Division I, then directed the team out of the arena and onto the bus.

"It's tremendously exciting," Spiotti said, boarding the Greyhound. "I thought for sure, with the way we approached it, that we'd be competitive (after the move to Division I five years earlier). But to be here in the Frozen Four is beyond my wildest dreams."

The bus's electronic scroll read: "RIT Hockey. Who are these guys?" "I put it in real quick," said driver Jim McKay. "I thought it was very appropriate." Very appropriate, indeed.

At the following day's press conferences, it was

Detroit native and RIT center Cameron Burt (18) prepares for a faceoff in the 2010 NCAA semifinals against Wisconsin.

apparent that the RIT hockey team had become media darlings. The team featured no shortage of compelling story lines. Among them, the tale of Cameron Burt, a Detroit native and one of the few African-Americans playing college hockey. He was all ready to attend Wayne State University in the Motor City, but had a change of plans when his hometown school dropped its hockey program before his freshman year. "It's a dream to be able to come back home to play in the Frozen Four," he said. "I feel very fortunate. It's a great opportunity." The native of Northwest Detroit was introduced to the game at the age of five because his dad "didn't want us to just play traditional African-American sports, like football and basketball. He wanted us to try something different, so he took us to a hockey game and we said, 'We'll try this.'"

The Tigers had drawn a tough assignment in their semifinal game. The University of Wisconsin Badgers were six-time national champions and had led the nation in scoring during the 2009–10 season with 163 goals. They had 11 National Hockey League draft picks on their roster, including two Hobey Baker Award college-player-of-the-year finalists—Blake Geoffrion and Brendan Smith. RIT did not have a single player on its roster who had been drafted by an NHL team, though defenseman Chris Tanev would wind up signing following the Frozen Four. Despite the daunting odds and the decided talent gap, Jared DeMichiel remained confident. He entered the semifinals as the nation's hottest goalie with a 27–9–1 won-lost record, a 1.98 goals-against average and a 92.4 save percentage. He had been even better in the post-season, going 4–0 and allowing just a goal per game, while stopping 96.6 percent of the shots he faced. Asked about RIT's underdog role, the colorful DeMichiel quipped: "I don't care if we are underdog, overdog or Snoop Dog."

Wilson had done a masterful job of guiding the motivated young men on his hockey team. He understood the challenges they faced in such a rigorous academic environment, and he made sure they fully enjoyed this once-in-a-lifetime journey they had embarked on.

"They have a lot of demands placed on their time between academics and hockey," he said. "But I don't want them to be so stressed that they lose the joy of the moment. I want them to have fun. I want them to soak in everything because for the vast majority of these kids, this will be the highlight of their competitive hockey careers, the zenith."

His players clearly enjoyed playing for him.

"He's one of the boys," Burt said. "But he's also like a second dad. He would do anything for us and we'd do anything for him."

Cornacchia echoed those sentiments, saying, "He's an invaluable asset to us. He means everything to this program." Wilson's deft mentoring of his student-athletes was not lost on RIT President Bill Destler. "Wayne is the perfect fit for the job," he said. "He cares about his players, and how they are doing both in school and on the ice."

Dan Ringwald earned All-American honors in 2009-10.

One person who took particular pride in the job Wilson had done was former RIT president, Al Simone. Not only had Simone signed off on Lou Spiotti's recommendation to hire Wilson, but he also was the man who entrusted Wilson with the task of shepherding RIT into the occasionally corrupt world of Division I athletics. Simone had not had a great experience with big-time college sports in his previous job as chancellor at the University of Hawaii. And that is why he initially refused to make the move from Division III to Division I after taking over the leadership of RIT. But he and the

Board of Trustees eventually decided it would be a good move for the school's men's hockey program because the schools in the American Hockey Association had a mission of academic integrity similar to the one that RIT boasted. Simone realized it would be a tough go for Wilson because the Tigers would not be offering athletic scholarships.

> I thought we would be competitive, and be contenders eventually. But not within five years (of changing divisions.) Credit him, Wayne Wilson. I admire his coaching and motivational ability, his personal example, and his focus on recruiting students who are academically oriented and who can play well under a team concept.

When asked about his philosophy, Wilson cited a book by former North Carolina basketball coaching legend Dean Smith. He told the *New York Times,*

> It's probably the book that's influenced me the most as a coach. I used to focus on, "Geez, we need to win this game. I hope we don't lose." It was always about winning and losing and the book kind of taught me that it's a process. We're not nervous about whether we win or lose a game. We're just trying to get better.

Wilson compared his team's improbable run to the one made by an underdog Butler team in the NCAA basketball tournament. Though not considered a basketball powerhouse, Butler shocked the college basketball world by reaching the Final Four, where it barely lost to Duke in the 2010 national championship game. "When you're in the heat of the moment, you think this is deserving," Wilson told the *Times* a few days before the Frozen Four. "But when you sit back, we've got to pinch ourselves a little bit, and say, 'Wow!'"

Although the Tigers were at a disadvantage because they didn't offer athletic scholarships, they did have more roster stability because their players weren't jumping to the NHL after their freshman or sophomore years. "That's a major factor," Wilson said of his team's success in 2009–10. "If you look at the elite programs, how many

Opposite: A crowd of 34,954 fans – the most ever to watch an RIT sporting event – showed up at Ford Field for the 2010 NCAA semifinal game between the Tigers and Wisconsin.

Left: RIT players are riveted to the action during their 2010 Frozen Four game vs. Wisconsin.

of their guys are leaving early—that's kind of leveling out the playing field for us because we're getting four-year players. We've got experience, and I think there's something to be said for that."

In the days before busing to the Motor City, Wilson reflected on how his team had already exceeded its expectations.

> Our goal this year was to get to the NCAAs. That was upfront, the very first meeting we had. We wanted to do a little bit better than the teams before us have done. Hopefully, we can set the bar that no other RIT team can beat.

The Frozen Four in April 2010 was to be played on Ford Field, the eight-year-old, $430-million stadium in downtown Detroit that was home to the NFL's Lions. The roofed-arena seated 80,000 spectators, making it roughly 40 times larger than RIT's hockey home, Ritter Arena. The rink was placed in one end zone instead of on the 50-yard line to improve the spectators' sight lines. NCAA officials were anticipating a crowd in excess of 30,000. The largest crowd for a home RIT sporting event to that point had been the 7,421 fans that had shown up for a men's hockey game eight months earlier at the Blue Cross Arena in downtown Rochester for a Brick City Homecoming game. "It was quite a spectacle, to play a game in a building as large as Ford Field," Wilson said. "I think we played in front of more people that day than we had in all of our home games combined that year."

Many of the 34,954 fans who showed up at Ford Field on April 8, 2010, and millions more who had tuned

The Tigers salute the fans following their 8-1 loss to Wisconsin in the 2010 NCAA semifinals.

in on ESPN2's national telecast, had hoped to see RIT's Cinderella story continue. The viewers included more than 2,000 orange-clad fans who were watching the game on a Jumbotron in Gordon Field House back on campus. Among the revelers was RITchie, the RIT mascot, who wore a T-shirt reading: "I eat Badgers for lunch."

On this day, though, Badgers would dine on Tigers, as RIT's dream season came to a crashing halt in an 8–1 blowout loss to Wisconsin. Wisconsin dominated from the get-go, outshooting RIT 37–14, in the most lop-sided game in the Frozen Four in 41 years. *Democrat and Chronicle* sportswriter Kevin Oklobzija captured the moment in his lede beneath the headline, "Abrupt Ending," in the next morning's newspaper.

"The Tigers weren't just swatted off their magic carpet," he wrote. "They were steamrolled and unceremoniously sent back to Henrietta by a vastly superior opponent." Senior defenseman Dan Ringwald couldn't argue with that assessment. "They definitely brought it," he said. "They played a great game, no question about it, and we didn't play our best." Wilson was philosophical in his post-game news conference. "Hey, we just ran into a powerhouse," he said. "They had an answer for everything. Physically, they were stronger, quicker." Cameron Burt, the Detroit native, took the loss harder than most. "Whenever you lose a game of this magnitude, it's hard to handle," said the sophomore, who was the Tigers' scoring leader that season with 16 goals and 31 assists. "You don't want to take your gear off because you know you're not going to put it on again this season."

Wisconsin served notice early that this was going to be their day, scoring just one minute and 27 seconds into the game on a rebound goal by John Mitchell. It marked the first time in 40 days that RIT had trailed in a game. Eight minutes later, Derek Stephen put the Badgers up 2–0. Wisconsin scored four more goals in the second period to turn the game into a rout. Tyler Brenner helped RIT avert being shut out when he scored on a power play with 28 seconds remaining in the second period.

DeMichiel, who went from torrid to as cold as the ice he was skating on, was under constant barrage from the fast-skating, hard-shooting Badgers. He managed to turn away 27 shots, but it was the eight he couldn't stop that obviously doomed RIT. "I don't think the score is indicative of our team whatsoever," he said afterward.

Ringwald, who was a second-team All-American, attempted to put things into perspective after the decisive defeat. "To make history for RIT is pretty special," he said. Those sentiments were echoed by senior left wing Stevan Matic. "Right now, it's kind of difficult to appreciate it," he said. "But I think in a week or so, we'll realize what we accomplished as a team, as individuals, for the school and for our conference, and it will feel a little sweeter." Wisconsin coach Mike Eaves sought out Wilson after the game to congratulate him on a marvelous season. "I said to Wayne he should be proud of what he did with that group of hockey people, bringing them together and having a good group of hockey players go to another level as a team to make themselves a threat," he said. "Not only to get here, but to put us in a game where we had to battle extremely hard." Wilson appreciated his

The Tigers make their way to the Ford Field ice.

counterpart's comments. "The score of the game was irrelevant to me," he said. "You lose, you lose. I'm just really proud. I mean, who would have ever thought that we could go this far, and how many other teams would rather be in our position, just to get to this point."

Several hundred fans greeted the team bus when it pulled onto campus the afternoon following the game. "We're showing them that we're here with them, win or lose," Jessica Rought told the *Democrat and Chronicle*. Wilson, who would wind up being named college hockey's coach of the year in a vote of his peers, thanked the crowd, adding that the fan support was something he'd cherish for the rest of his life. President Destler then took the microphone and shouted, "What a ride! What a ride!" He praised Wilson and the players "for everything you did for this campus," adding, "You represented us so wonderfully. This team brought a sense of school spirit and excitement that will be hard to match."

GARBOWSKY GAVE FANS A PARTING GIFT TO REMEMBER

Absence definitely made Matt Garbowsky's heart grow fonder. After missing 24 games during his junior season with a broken wrist, the Canadian forward came back with a vengeance during his senior campaign (2014-15). He established a new school Division I record for most goals (26) and points (54) in a season, while leading the nation in face-off victories (729). His exploits did not go unnoticed as he was named one of 10 finalists for college hockey's most prestigious honor – the Hobey Baker Award – as well as the Atlantic Hockey Conference player and defender of the year. "Matt Garbowsky is the most complete player I've had the opportunity to coach here at RIT," said Tigers head coach Wayne Wilson. "Being named conference player of the year is a great honor, but being named defensive player of the year while leading the conference in both goals and points says everything you need to know about Matt's game."

The humble young man who was known to his coaches and teammates as "Garbo" acknowledged that missing most of his junior year gave him a deeper appreciation for the game and motivated him to not take anything for granted during his final season of college hockey. When he began racking up the individual honors, he was quick to compliment his teammates, particularly linemates Josh Mitchell and Brad McGowan. "It's nice to be recognized, but I'm just trying to play my game and keep producing with my line," he said, when he was informed about being a Baker finalist. "It's a team game and I wouldn't be recognized without my teammates helping me."

Following his final college game, Garbowsky signed a professional contract with the Rochester Americans, the top minor league affiliate of the Buffalo Sabres of the National Hockey League.

WHEN DAVID BEAT GOLIATH

Although RIT's 2014-15 season ended one game shy of a return trip to the NCAA Frozen Four, Tigers fans will always have fond memories of the campaign's second-to-last game. That contest saw their team become the first 16th seed in tournament history to knock off the No. 1 seed. Josh Mitchell scored the winning goal with just under six minutes remaining and goalie Jordan Ruby turned away 33 of 34 shots as the Tigers pulled off their most monumental upset – a 2-1 victory vs. top-ranked Minnesota State. It marked the first time the tournament's bottom seed has defeated the No. 1 seed and also the first time in RIT's then-10-year Division I history it had beaten the nation's No. 1 team. Alexander Kuqali put the Tigers on top, scoring four minutes and thirty seconds into the contest. Minnesota tied it when Teddy Blueger rifled a shot past Ruby in the second period. That would be the only goal allowed by the senior goaltender, who helped ignite a late-season charge by the Tigers that would see them win eight of their final nine games, including four straight in the Atlantic Hockey Conference tournament to earn their second NCAA berth at the Division I level. The run came to an end in the Midwest Regional finals with a 4-0 loss to the University of Nebraska/Omaha. But when fans look back at RIT's 20-15-5 record from that season, they'll focus on that night in South Bend, Indiana when the Tigers made college hockey history.

NCAA
RIT
BAUER

6.

THE WOMEN WIN IT ALL

During its first two decades of existence, the RIT women's program could best be described as stuck in neutral, producing 13 losing records and only six winning seasons. It wasn't until the brother coaching combo of Rick and Bob Filighera took over in 1995 that things began changing for the better. Natives of the Buffalo suburb of Hamburg, each had enjoyed college hockey playing success—Rick at Brockport State, Bob at Buffalo State—and scholastic coaching success—Rick at Brockport High School, where he guided the boys to a sectional title, and Bob at Frontier High School, where he won a league championship. In addition to his high school assignment, Rick also had experienced success coaching both boys' and girls' youth league hockey teams. Led by junior defenseman and captain Shelley Moore, and a host of new recruits, RIT rebounded from a 6–11 record in 1994–95 to a 13–4–1 record—the best in school history—in Rick Filighera's first season in 1995–96. From that moment forward, the women's team reeled off 20 consecutive winning seasons. The Tigers went 35–15–5 in the seasons under the Filigheras, and would become even more dominating under their successor, Rob Scuteri, who would guide RIT to a 78–28–14 record in his five seasons as coach. Mike Grainsky took over in 2003, and in three seasons, led the team to a 49–26–3 mark.

Although the RIT women's program had enjoyed unprecedented success under those three coaching staffs, it wasn't until Scott McDonald took over in 2006 that the Tigers established themselves as a national powerhouse. McDonald had grown up in the Toronto suburb of Oakville, Ontario, and like that of many Canadian boys, his youth was spent chasing pucks on ice.

> I have fond, fond memories of watching Hockey Night in Canada with my family on Saturday nights—that was a big tradition. And I vividly remember skating on the ice all the time. Hockey pretty much was life. I guess that's the easiest way of putting it.

His exploits in youth travel hockey leagues caught the attention of former RIT star Blaise MacDonald, who was coaching at Niagara University and convinced

Opposite: The 2011-12 women's hockey team proudly displays its NCAA Division III championship trophy.

Coach Scott McDonald is the winningest coach in RIT women's hockey history.

McDonald to come play for the Purple Eagles. The experience was a good one for McDonald. During his senior season in 2000, the gifted defenseman helped Niagara post a 30–8–4 record and earn an NCAA tournament berth in just the school's fourth year as a Division I program. After graduating with a degree in communications studies, McDonald played professionally—first with the San Angelo (Texas) Outlaws of the Western Professional Hockey League, then with a team in the Swedish Hockey League. "After two years of that, I knew it was time to move on, that I didn't have a future as a player," he said. "Even when I was playing junior hockey, I knew that I wanted to coach one day. My dad had been a coach and the idea of doing that as a career was cemented in my mind when I attended a hockey camp at the University of Michigan, run by Red Berenson. Red had been a great player in the National Hockey League, who's gone on to become an even bigger legend as a college hockey coach at Michigan. That experience of meeting him during that camp and being on a college campus convinced me that college coaching was the path I'd eventually pursue."

When McDonald returned from playing in Sweden, a friend told him that Utica College was looking for an assistant men's hockey coach. McDonald applied and was hired. "It was a good experience, but it also was a real eye-opener," he said. "It was a lot harder than I anticipated. I discovered that coaches have it a lot rougher than players. When you're a player, you show up for practice and games and that's that. But coaches are always on the clock. And at that level, you're doing it all. Besides practices and games, you're on the road a lot recruiting, you're making travel arrangements for away games, dealing with parents, fixing and ordering equipment, etc. So that first year was quite a shock."

A shock, indeed, but also great and necessary preparation for becoming a head coach. During his travels, he would occasionally run into RIT men's head coach, Wayne Wilson.

> I made sure I introduced myself to Wayne because he was such a respected coach and he ran a model program at RIT. One of the reasons he's so respected isn't just the wins and losses, but his willingness to help out young and up-and-coming coaches. It doesn't matter if you are a coach at the highest level of college hockey or an unknown assistant, Wayne is the type of guy who always makes time for people in his profession. He goes out of his way to give back.

During their conversations, McDonald made sure to point out that his wife was from Rochester.

> I was kind of planting the seed, you know, just in case there was an opening at RIT down the road. Wayne and I hit it off right away, but I never expected the opportunity to come as soon as it did. The following year, I was working for Wayne. It was the best thing that ever happened to me, career-wise.

From 2003 to 2006, McDonald learned at the side of a master coach. Wilson liked McDonald's work ethic and hockey knowledge, and entrusted him with much of the recruiting as RIT made the transition from Division III to Division I. "Scott worked his tail off for us," Wilson said. "He played a big role in helping us make that big leap."

One of McDonald's side jobs was managing the ice time at Ritter Arena. That included making sure the rink was ready for RIT women's practices and games. Little did he know the time spent watching them play and practice would help prepare him for his next job.

> I had a lot of time to kill, so I would observe what was going on out there, and I got to know some of the women players because some of them were dating the men's hockey players. I just observed and listened, but I didn't offer my two cents. But in my mind, I guess I was thinking how I might run their practices and games, and how I might try to motivate them. That wasn't meant as a knock on their coaches. It's just something I guess every coach or would-be coach would do subconsciously.

McDonald also got a taste of what it would be like to coach women's hockey during summer camps he worked at other colleges. After one camp at Hamilton College, in which he spent time coaching both men's and women's players, a friend told McDonald he would be a natural coaching a women's team at the college level. "His comment kind of caught me by surprise," McDonald said. "I had never entertained that idea."

After Michael Grainsky stepped down following the 2005–06 hockey season, the women's position opened up, and McDonald recalled his friend's comment. He began assessing his career and his life.

> There were a lot of things going on. My wife had a very good job at a local hospital and we were thinking about starting a family, so moving on to another job in the next few years wasn't appealing. I knew Wayne wasn't going anywhere, so if I wanted to be a head coach, it probably wasn't going to happen with the men's program. So, I started thinking about the women's program. It would enable me to realize my dream of becoming a head coach. It would be a jump in pay. (For the first time in program history, it would be a full-time position.) And I already knew how we did things at RIT, and I had at least some familiarity with the women's team, so it all started to make sense. I spoke to Wayne about it, and he was all for it. And I spoke to (athletic director) Lou Spiotti about it, and he was very supportive. He encouraged me to go through the application and interview process. He told me that even if I didn't get the job, I would benefit from the experience.

Spiotti's search committee came back with a glowing review of McDonald.

> I liked Scott from the start and thought he would be a great candidate, but I removed myself from the initial search process because I wanted the committee to do an objective job," said Spiotti. "I'll play devil's advocate with them in any coaching search we do. I'll challenge them, even though in most cases, they come back with the person I believe is the right person for the job. And that was the case with Scott. I agreed 100 percent with the committee that he was the perfect person to take our women's program to the next level.

McDonald didn't waste any time making an impact. Inheriting a team that had gone 15–10 the year before, he guided the Tigers to a school-record 22 wins in his first season at the helm as the RIT women earned their first NCAA tournament invitation.

> Being able to watch them from afar for three years, while I was managing the rink, gave me a good feeling for the program and what needed to be done. I thought they could probably work harder and compete harder. I felt they needed to be challenged. I told them right from the first day that if they wanted to be a championship contender rather than remain mediocre, they were going to have to do things differently than they had before. I think they bought into what we were preaching, and all of a sudden the wins began piling up.

There was an adjustment period at first, for both coach and players. McDonald described how he made the transition.

> There are slight differences between coaching men and coaching women, but there are more similarities than people might think. I've always taken the approach of looking at whomever I'm coaching as hockey players, not as guy hockey players or girl hockey players. And I think our players responded to that. I pushed them just as hard as I had pushed the guys. When I look at them, I see hockey helmets and masks. I don't see the ponytails coming out of the back of the helmet.

McDonald's players came to appreciate that. "Scott said if we wanted to be respected like the men's program was, we needed to work as hard they did," said Kristina Moss, who would go on to establish herself as one of the greatest players in school history. "The fact that he didn't treat us like little girls, but rather as hockey players, was the best thing that could have happened to us. He pushed us to be the best, and, as a result got the best out of all of us."

Under McDonald, the bar had been raised dramatically. After that first NCAA appearance, in which RIT lost in the opening round to Amherst, the expectations were for a Division III national championship. Achieving that goal would not come easily. During the next three seasons, the Tigers would establish themselves as an up-and-coming hockey power, posting a combined 59–15–5 record, but they failed to return to the NCAA tournament. McDonald continued to work hard, especially in the area of recruiting, and when the Tigers took the ice for the 2010–11 season, he felt that he had put together a team talented enough to win it all. Paced by All-Americans Sarah Dagg and Katie Stack, they posted a 26–2–2 record and made it to their first NCAA title game. But the sterling

Defenseman Kristina Moss was named an NCAA All-American in 2011-12.

season ended in bitter disappointment as Norwich stunned RIT, 5–2, at Ritter Arena. The post-game ceremonies from that night remain seared in Moss' memory.

> It was awful having to stand out there on the ice for 20 minutes and watch the Norwich players skate around our rink holding up the national championship trophy. We had had such an incredible run, and it was all laid out there for us to finish things with a championship in front of our family and friends. And then Norwich went out and ruined the party for us. We didn't play a good game and Norwich did. I still don't like to think about that game.

Neither does McDonald.

> To say it was devastating would be putting it lightly. That team was loaded with talent—we had three All-Americans and several other players who would become All-Americans in the years that followed. And they had played so well throughout the season. We had just beaten Middlebury the day before, and that was a huge step for us, because they were a team we had had a tough time against in previous years. Plus, we were playing the championship game on our home ice, which was a huge advantage. So, it was all there for us, on a silver platter.

But Norwich, which had lost in the championship game the year before, played with a greater hunger. McDonald felt he was at fault.

SHE'S GLAD SHE SWITCHED

Sarah Dagg

Sarah Dagg started out in figure skating, but quickly became bored. One day, after watching one of her older brother's hockey games in their hometown of St. George, Ontario, Canada, she decided to give that sport a shot. Rifling pucks into the net proved much more enjoyable than trying to land triple lutzes. Dagg wound up dominating her hockey competition, first on her high school girls' team, and then in juniors, where she earned high-scorer and tournament most valuable player honors at the prestigious Ontario Winter Games. Her swift skating and deft stick-handling caught the attention of RIT Coach Scott McDonald. Dagg liked the program's track record of success and the fact that campus was only about a 90-minute drive from her home, meaning her parents would be able to make the trip for many of her games.

Although she maxed out at five feet, two inches tall, Dagg wound up casting a huge shadow at RIT. By the time her collegiate playing career was over, she had established herself as the school's all-time points (154) and assists (91) leader. The hospitality major saved her best for last, finishing fourth nationally in scoring with 18 goals and 24 assists during the 2010–11 season as the Tigers reached the national championship game for the first time. Dagg's play captured the attention of the nation's hockey coaches, who voted her the 2011 winner of the Laura Hurd Award, presented annually to the top player in Division III. "Sarah was the heart and soul of the team all four years she played here," McDonald said. "She brought an energy level and work ethic to every practice, every game, that was unmatched." Dagg and teammate Katie Stack wound up being drafted to play in a Canadian professional hockey league after they graduated from RIT.

> I put the full blame on myself, because, in hindsight, I had allowed our team to think it was a foregone conclusion, that we were going to win the game just by showing up. Going into the locker room before the game, I noticed how we were oddly quiet. The music, which usually was blasting, wasn't on. We were normally a very outgoing team, but everybody seemed tense. Nobody was singing or joking around. That concerned me. But I tried not to read too much into it. I said to myself, "Okay, let's just get through the first five minutes and get through the jitters, and we'll be back to being the team we've been all season."

Not long after the opening face-off, the Tigers found themselves on a two-on-one break.

"Sarah Dagg, our player of the year, slides the puck over to our leading scorer, Kolbee McCrea, and she completely misses the net with her shot," McDonald recalled. "If she scores in that first 30 seconds of the game, the roof would have come off the building, and we would have been able to relax and get back to normal. But she misses badly on the shot and then Norwich comes down with the puck and scores on their first shot. I'm still optimistic because we were a high-scoring team. But they scored again about a minute later. We fought back to make it 3–2 at the end of the first period, but they scored another goal in the second, and, although we totally outplayed them in that period, we couldn't find the net. They added another in the final period and we never got untracked."

One of the things that bothered McDonald most was the impact of the loss on his seniors, especially Dagg and Stack, who would wind up being drafted to play women's professional hockey.

> They were part of my first recruiting class, and I told them, 'You guys will make the difference; we'll be a national contender if you come to RIT.' Well, they held up their end of the bargain. They did everything we asked them to do—and more. We had the Cinderella story going until Norwich stole our slippers.

Although their graduation left a huge void, McDonald was confident that his corps of returning players, along with an influx of talented incoming freshman, would enable RIT to contend again in 2011–12. As painful as the loss to Norwich was, McDonald didn't want his returning players to forget about it. He intended to use it as a motivational ploy. And that explains why he put the runners-up trophy on prominent display in his office. Kim Schlattman, the captain of that year's team, saw it repeatedly.

> You couldn't miss it. Every time you went in to talk to coach it was there in full view—a reminder of how close we had come to winning it all. And when we were sluggish in practices, Scott would ask us if we were interested in experiencing the pain we had of finishing second or if we wanted to experience the joy of what it felt like to win it all. It definitely worked.

It did, indeed. The Tigers started the season with a vengeance. They opened with a decisive 6–3 victory over Manhattanville (New York) College on October 28, 2011, then crushed Norwich, 4–1, the next night. That would start them on a 14–0 roll. The top-ranked Tigers

Katie Stack earned All-American honors twice for the Tigers.

then bused north for a two-game series against another Division III powerhouse, Plattsburgh. Their luck would run out on Friday, January 13. That night the teams played to a 1–1 overtime tie. The next night, Plattsburgh snapped RIT's unbeaten streak with a 3–1 victory. In retrospect, McDonald thought the loss was a win.

> Looking back, that was the best thing that could have happened to us. People had already been talking about whether we'd be able to run the table and go the entire season without a loss. I don't think we were cocky, heading up there that weekend, but I think we getting close to thinking that we could just show up and win. We got humbled very quickly. That forced us to step back and assess things. It also removed the pressure of going undefeated. That hadn't been our goal anyway. Our goal was to win the championship.

After that lost weekend in the North Country, the Tigers regained their focus, and went on another 14-game win streak. McDonald liked the way his team was meshing, on and off the ice. "It was a close-knit team," said Schlattman, the junior forward whom the players had voted captain before the season opener.

> There were four houses that most of the players lived in, so we were always hanging out together— either there, or in the classroom, or the ice. We had a wide range of personalities. There were people like our goalie, Laura Chamberlain, who was very quiet, and there were people on the other end of the spectrum, like Tenecia Hiller

> and Ali Hills and Carley King, who were very outgoing. Everyone was so different, which I think made for a great mix. No one butted heads. Everyone got along. We were just like one big family. You really couldn't avoid each other, but we didn't want to.

Hockey players can be quite superstitious, and as the season progressed the Tigers developed a number of routines they religiously followed. "We didn't want to tempt the fates," Schlattman joked. "Everyone sat in a particular seat on the bus during road games, and when we went to a restaurant, we would sit in the same order at the table." That season they became obsessed with the popular television show about the intensity of big-time Texas high school football, called *Friday Night Lights.*

"We would watch it during bus trips,"Schlattman said. "I think we went through every episode of the series by the time we were halfway through our season. We adopted the motto of the Panthers, the team that was featured in the series. They had this slogan: 'Clear eyes, full hearts, can't lose.' We put those words up in our locker room and had sweatshirts made up that had the words "clear eyes, full hearts" on the front and "can't lose" on the back."

Before taking the ice for each game at Ritter Arena, the players huddled in the middle of the locker room and swayed to a song called "Turbulence." When the song concluded, one player would shout: "Clear eyes!" Another would follow with: "Full hearts!" And the whole team would chant, in unison, "Can't lose!" as they stormed out of the room and through the tunnel to the rink. "I know it sounds a little strange," Moss said. "But it did help us stay focused, so we stuck to our routines."

On Sunday, March 4, the Tigers avenged their loss to Plattsburgh with a 2–1 win in the ECAC West title game to maintain their No.1 ranking in the Division III national polls and earn the No. 1 seed in the 2012 NCAA hockey tournament. RIT easily won its opening-round game against Concordia College from Minnesota, 5–2, as Kolbee McCrea scored three goals. The thing Schlattman remembers most about that night wasn't McCrea's hat trick, but her unplanned haircut.

> Kolbee had really long hair, which she tied into a ponytail. There was a play during the game when she fell to the ice and a girl from the other team skated by and accidentally cut about six inches off Kolbee's ponytail. They actually stopped the game so they could get her chunk of hair off the ice so nobody would trip over it. We had a good time joking with her about that one. We asked her if the girl who had skated over her ponytail was going to charge her for the haircut. And we joked that the girl on the Concordia team who did that to her should get two minutes in the penalty box for slashing.

The victory set up yet another pressure-packed game with Plattsburgh in the NCAA semifinals. The teams had split their first three matchups that season, but this game on March 16, 2012 would determine more than bragging rights. It would determine which team would advance to the national championship game. Although the game was being played in front of the RIT faithful at Ritter Arena, Schlattman was nervous.

ALL-AMERICANS

Here is a list of RIT female hockey players who have earned All-American honors:

Colleen Baude	2001–02
Jen Gorczynski	2001–02, '02–03, '03–04
Stacey McConnell	2006–07
Danielle Nagymarosi	2006–07
Sarah Dagg	2008–09, '09–10, '10–11
Erica Owczarczak	2008–09
Katie Stack	2009–10, '10–11
Traci Galbraith	2010–11
Kristina Moss	2011–12
Laura Chamberlain	2011–12
Kourtney Kunichika	2011–12
Ali Binnington	2013–14

> We already had played three exhausting, down-to-the-wire games with them, so I was concerned. I felt we could win, but I knew we were evenly matched and if the puck bounced the wrong way in a game like this, you could find yourself on the short end of the scoreboard.

As had been the case in their earlier meetings, this one was a nail-biter. The Tigers scored first on a goal by Marissa Maugeri, and Laura Chamberlain's superb goal-tending made the lead hold up until Emma Rutherford swatted a puck by her to tie the game with five minutes remaining in the third period. Neither team scored again in regulation, meaning the game would be decided in overtime. After the Tigers returned to the locker room while the Zamboni cleared the ice for the extra period, Schlattman addressed her teammates.

> I told them: "Don't worry, girls. We've got this one. Laura is playing great. And we're going to go out there and get a goal in OT and win this thing." But, in reality, my stomach was churning and I was panicking, even though I was trying my best not to show it. After I got done with my little pep talk, I said to myself, "God, please don't let us lose this game. We've come too far and worked so hard to get here." This would be harder to swallow than losing in the title game last year.

Schlattman's prayers wound up being answered. Two minutes and 30 seconds after the overtime began, freshman defenseman Lindsay Grigg scored one of the biggest goals in RIT history, rifling a cross-ice pass from Ariane Yokoyama past Plattsburgh goaltender Sydney Aveson, for a 2–1 victory. Grigg's goal was the highlight of the night, but RIT's second trip to the title game in as many years would not have been possible without Chamberlain's scintillating play. The sophomore from Norco, California stopped 33 shots, several of which came while RIT was forced to play a woman down during five penalties. "When Lindsay scored that goal, I felt as if a boulder had been removed from my shoulders," Schlattman said. "And, unlike my feelings heading into the Plattsburgh game, I felt calm and confident that we were going to win it all the next night." As fate would have it, Norwich won its semifinal game, setting up the matchup the Tigers had desired for more than a year. "It all unfolded the way we wanted," Moss said. "Now, we just had to complete the deal."

All-American Kourtney Kunichika (left) celebrates her goal during RIT's 4-1 victory against Norwich in the 2012 NCAA Division III title game.

The year before, the RIT players had spent the eve of the championship game in a hotel with the other Final Four teams. McDonald asked his players if they wanted to do the same thing this time around and they said, "No." "We wanted to do things differently, so we could come up with a different result," Schlattman said. "And that's why we told Coach we'd be better off if we slept in our own beds, and he agreed." When Schlattman and her teammates arrived at Ritter that afternoon, the captain could sense that they were a lot looser than they had been the year before.

Coach McDonald asked me and Kristina to make sure we followed the routines we had followed before each of the other games that season. And he told me to make sure our music was blaring. He didn't want silence the way it had been the year before. He wanted us to go about this the way we had every game. Even though this was biggest game of our lives, he didn't want us to think about it that way because he knew if we did our nerves would get the better of us, just like they had a year earlier.

Celeste Brown scores what proves to be the decisive goal in the 2012 championship game vs. Norwich.

Before the Tigers took the ice for the opening face-off, they huddled in the middle of the locker room and swayed back and forth to their adopted theme song, "Turbulence." When that was over, they followed their *Friday Night Lights* ritual in which they did their "Clear eyes, full hearts, can't lose" chant. And then they rumbled through the tunnel and onto the ice to thunderous applause from the more than 1,000 spectators, including hundreds of members of the Corner Crew.

Moss put the Tigers ahead, 1–0, when she fired a shot that deflected off a Norwich player and into the goal nine minutes and six seconds into the game. Five minutes later, the visitors tied the score, but RIT took control of the game on goals by Celeste Brown, Kourtney Kunichika and Ali Hills during a 10-minute span in the final period. That helped the Tigers relax, according to Moss.

> I think scoring first took a lot of the pressure off of us. The year before, we fell behind and panicked. Even though Norwich came back and tied it, we felt in control.

When the horn sounded on RIT's 4–1 victory, the players jumped over the bench and formed a pile on top of Chamberlain, who had made 27 saves and was named the Final Four's Most Outstanding Player. "It's an unreal feeling," Moss told reporters afterward. "I can't even explain it. I'm on cloud nine."

This time, unlike the year before, Moss and her teammates were more than happy to remain on the ice for the awards ceremonies. Queen's song "We Are the Champions" blared over the loudspeakers as the Tigers took turns holding up the first national championship trophy won by an RIT women's team in any sport. Moss was delighted.

> I still get chills just thinking about it. People ask me how long it took for me to get over the loss to

The Tigers celebrate their 2012 national championship victory.

> Norwich the year before and I told them, it took me an entire year. I really didn't get over it until we beat them in the championship game in 2012. Winning that championship was the greatest thrill of my life.

More than anything, McDonald felt a sense of relief. "We had worked so hard to get back to that game, and I probably would have jumped off a bridge if we had gone that far and blown it again," she said. The upperclassmen had come through for the Tigers, but so did the talented freshmen McDonald had recruited, including Grigg, who scored the game-winner the night before, and Celeste Brown, who had the decisive goal in the title game.

"It was a pretty emotional scene after we won, and the freshman players were among the most emotional," Schlattman said. "A few of them came up to me and said, 'We're so happy we could help you win this after all you guys went through the year before.' That was very touching."

Moss and Kunichika joined Chamberlain on the all-tournament team as RIT finished 28–1–1, establishing a new Division III record for most victories in a season. The three also would receive All-American honors. Kunichika, one of several Californians on the team, led the Tigers in scoring with 45 points, while Moss and Chamberlain helped RIT record eight shutouts while allowing an average of one goal per game, the best goals-against average in the nation. Chamberlain, Schlattman, and Melissa Bromley were named National Scholars by the American Women Coaches Hockey Association. All the players and coaches received honorary keys to the city from Rochester Mayor Tom Richards.

SUPERLATIVES FROM WOMEN'S 2011–12 TITLE SEASON

28 wins, an NCAA Division III women's hockey record

Just 30 goals allowed in 30 games

147 goals scored, almost five per game

15 consecutive wins at Ritter Arena

Two 14-game win streaks—one to open the season, one to end it

Nine of the 23 players on the roster earned ECAC West All-Academic honors

Three players—Kourtney Kunichika, Laura Chamberlain and Kristina Moss—earned All-American honors

Played Plattsburgh State four times, beating them twice, losing once and tying once

"It was the most unbelievable experience," Moss said. "And just when we didn't think it could get any better, it did." Just three days after their momentous victory, the players were called to a special meeting and informed that the women's hockey program would be competing in Division I the next season. Schlattman recalled their reaction.

> We were in shock at first. We had heard rumors that the school might go DI in women's hockey, but we didn't think it would happen as quickly as it did. Between winning it all, then learning we were going to get a chance to be a part of the first team to go Division I made for a couple of surreal weeks.

McDonald had known about the news since early January, but had asked athletic director Lou Spiotti to keep it a secret until after the season was over.

"I had been a part of the transition when I was with the men's program and we announced it early in the season that we were going Division I the following year and it totally distracted our team," McDonald explained. "That team lost its focus for the rest of the year and wound up underachieving on the ice. So, knowing that, I asked Lou if we could play the year out before holding the press conference, and he was all for that."

The timing couldn't have been better, because literally a few hours before the press conference, Spiotti learned that Niagara University was dropping its women's hockey program and College Hockey America officials called to see if RIT could take the Purple Eagles' spot in 2012–13. "We'd be able to start out in a league rather than as an independent, so our scheduling problems

While winning the school's first women's national championship, the 2012 Tigers also established an NCAA record for most wins in a season (28).

were taken care of," McDonald said.

The Tigers didn't waste any time showing they were up to the task of competing at the highest level of intercollegiate women's hockey. That first season, they went a respectable 16–16–5 against schools that, unlike RIT, offered athletic scholarships. Year Two was even better as the Tigers won 11 of the their final 18 games to win the CHA championship, 2–1, in double overtime against Mercyhurst, which had beaten them in their first Division I game two years earlier.

Although they suffered a slew of injuries and slipped to a 15-19-5 record during the 2014-15 season, the Tigers got hot at the right time, winning seven of eight games down the stretch, including four straight in the College Hockey America tournament, to claim their second consecutive league title and earn their first NCAA Division I post-season berth. Though they lost their opening round game, 6-2, to No. 1 University of Minnesota, it was a memorable season. The Tigers were offensively challenged, averaging just below two goals per game. But senior Ali Binnington kept them in most contests with superb goaltending. She missed 10 games with injuries, but still managed to finish her final season with a respectable 12-11-3 won-lost record, a 1.82 goals against average and five shutouts. The Canadian left RIT as the all-time leader in saves (2,292) and shutouts (19), while going 49-30-9 with a 1.73 goals against average.

Binnington was superb, even in defeat, making 46 saves in the loss to a superior Minnesota team. "I couldn't be prouder of the way we played," McDonald said after that game. "Minnesota is such a highly skilled team and they showed that on the power play, which was the difference. I thought our energy and effort was really strong. Today was a great stepping stone for our program."

A CHAMPIONSHIP TRADITION

The RIT men's team won a national championship in Division II in 1983 and in Division III in 1985. They reached the NCAA Final Four in Division III seven times (1984, '85, '86, '89, '96, '99, '01), Division II once (1983) and Division I once (2010). They've played in the NCAA tournament 14 times ('83, '85, '86, '89, '94, '96, '97, '98, '99, '00, '01, '02, '10, '15) and were ECAC West regular-season champs four times (2000, '01, '02, '03) and Atlantic Hockey Association regular-season champs four times (2007, '09, '10, '11).

The women's team won a national championship in Division III in 2011–12 and reached the Final Four one other time (2010–11) when they finished as national runners-up. They made two other NCAA tournament appearances in 2007 and 2015. They won the College Hockey America tournament in 2014 and 2015.

RIT President Bill Destler drops the puck for the ceremonial face-off before the women's first game as a Division I program in the fall of 2012.

CORNER CREW
WARNING: WE BE LOUD AND OBNOXIOUS AT HOCKEY GAMES!
got goalie?
i think not
ROPPONEN
HARTLEY
CORNACCHIA
SPIVAK

7.

WHAT A CREW!

Players and coaches have come and gone through the decades, but the one constant with the RIT hockey program has been the fan support. Like the Cameron Crazies at Duke University, Otto's Army at Syracuse and The Twelfth Man at Texas A&M, the Corner Crew—first at Ritter Arena, and now at the Gene Polisseni Center—has established itself as one of the most passionate and creative student/alumni cheering sections in all of college sports.

"I think when you look back at the history of our hockey teams, there's no question that the Corner Crew has contributed to our success," said long-time RIT athletics director Lou Spiotti of the group of fans who set up shop in the corners of the south end of the rink. "They've created an atmosphere that's certainly given us a home ice advantage, and helped us recruit a number of student athletes who wanted to play at a place where the fans take their hockey seriously."

Chris Lerch concurs. He holds undergraduate and graduate degrees from RIT, and for two decades he has been writing about the game for *U.S. College Hockey Online,* as well as providing radio color commentary on Tiger games.

> There's an enthusiasm and passion at RIT home hockey games that's missing at most professional games, and even at most college games. I know I might be considered biased because of my connection to RIT, but I've covered hockey at a lot of different places through the years, and the Corner Crew stacks up with any group of fans as far as enthusiasm and ingenuity.

The Crew's roots can be traced to the 1969–70 season, a year after Ritter opened on the Henrietta campus. According to John Henze, who graduated with a degree in fine and applied arts in 1974, he and several other students started a cheering section at men's hockey games his freshman year.

"We didn't have nearly as many followers as there are now," he wrote in a letter to *University Magazine* in the fall of 2011. "But I bet we were nearly as vocal. This was before the glass was put in all the way around the rink, and to be frank, we really got into the game. Sometimes

Opposite: RIT players acknowledge the Corner Crew student/alumni cheer section after a victory at Ritter Arena.

quite literally. Of course, the Corner Crew of today is much more organized than we were. Their cheers are better. They are a sight to behold, and be proud of, what with the matching jerseys and all. But we were the first to have shirts. We all wore T-shirts with a logo on it and we were very proud of it. As I am sure they all are now."

Henze said the shirts were light lavender. (He doesn't know why they picked that color instead of the school colors—orange and brown.)

> We wore them to every game just as they do today. They pretty much said this is our corner of the rink and don't you dare sit here. Ever!

Marty Reeners, a 1974 RIT graduate and former Tigers hockey player, also has vivid memories of the Corner Crew in its early years. He described them as

> a very active, boisterous and sometimes obnoxious fan club that attended every game and sat in that same corner. Our opponents often commented on how intimidating they were. They conducted organized cheers aimed at opposing goaltenders as well as the officials. Most of their activities were just spirited vocal support for a bunch of "walk on" players that loved the game and enjoyed playing in front of the students, families and friends.

Reeners recalled a game during the early 1970s when streaking was a fad on college campuses and about a dozen naked fraternity brothers streaked around the running track above the rink at Ritter before exiting to the cheers and squeals of the crowd.

> My father was sitting with my girlfriend, who would become my wife, near that level where the streaking was going on. That was a little awkward for her, my dad and me. But it was just a bunch of frat boys having some fun. No harm.

He remembers another night when there *was* some harm.

> A fan tossed a pop can and clocked the referee in the head. Play was stopped and the building was emptied. When we resumed play, there were maybe 15–20 people in the stands, mostly parents.

During the 1970s and into the early 1980s, two groups of vocal supporters occupied separate corners on the south side of Ritter. The southeast corner was made up largely of computer majors, as well as some faculty, staff and alumni. The southwest corner was made up of mostly photography students. Each group created chants they would use routinely. They often would scream in unison, "Put him in the box!" when an opposing player was called for a penalty, or "The ref is out to lunch!" when a call went against RIT. A number of the chants were profane, prompting school administrators to meet with student leaders in hopes of toning it down.

"The cheers weren't always G-rated," joked Steve Schultz, a legendary Corner Crew character, who became a major RIT benefactor and a member of the school's board of trustees. "In fact some of the stuff was crude, but things were a little different back in the day. Kids were just blowing off steam. It was a great stress-reliever."

Schultz, who earned his degree in computer science in 1989, saw cheering with the Corner Crew as one of the few extracurricular activities on campus that engendered school spirit.

THE RIT CORNER CREW:

Tiger Hockey's Die-Hard Fans

(center) The Grim Reaper leads the Corner Crew in demanding one more goal.

(far left) The T-shirt says it all.

(bottom right) The traditional post-goal headbutt is performed but two of the Corner's fanatics.

(below) The Tigers and their crowd celebrate victory over A.I.C.

Any time RIT's Hockey team is up against an opponent you will find a devoted backing of frenzied fans known simply as the Corner Crew. Although they have been criticized for their abusive tone toward the opponent, it is not uncommon to hear a cry of "Give it to a kid!" when the puck flies into the crowd. The Corner crew provides consistent moral support for the team as well as creating a psychological edge over the opposing team. Despite a decrease in fan attendance recently, this group of dedicated and highly spirited backers has shown their loyalty game after game from the corner of the rink.

PHOTOGRAPHS BY PAUL NISELY

8 19

A pictorial about the Corner Crew in the student newspaper, *The Reporter*.

It was a lot different climate on campus back in the 1980s. The school did not have a great student atmosphere back then the way it does now. RIT was viewed as a graduate factory. It was sort of a cold place. You pay me the money. I give you the degree. That was the one-sided nature of the place. I remember the summer before I showed up. I had been accepted and I was walking across campus with my mother and this student sees me and he shouts: "Don't go here. It's horrible. There's nothing to do. It's cold. It's a high-pressure environment." I was like, "Whoa! Maybe this isn't the place for me." There were extracurricular things to do back then, but you had to go find them. Fortunately, things have changed 180 degrees. There's much, much more out there as far as activities beyond the classroom, and the school does a better job of letting students know about them.

A Santa Claus on skates tosses candy to members of the Corner Crew.

Despite the obstacles, Schultz said he had a marvelous experience at RIT. He was involved with the school newspaper, academic fraternities and student government. But some of his fondest memories were spent as one of the leaders of the Corner Crew.

"It wasn't called that right away," he said. "We didn't have a formal name. It was just a bunch of like-minded people who hung out together and liked to be vocal at hockey games."

Schultz's identity and place in RIT hockey lore would forever be cemented on Halloween weekend 1982. Until that time, he was just another loud, at times obnoxious, Tigers fan. He blended into the crowd. After that weekend, he would become one of the most recognizable figures in the school's hockey history. He remembers it well.

The first game was on a Friday night, which happened to be Halloween, so a bunch of us decided to dress up in costumes and go to happy hour before heading over to the game. I chose the

Steve Schultz became part of RIT hockey lore as the Corner Crew's Grim Reaper.

> Grim Reaper for my costume and I wound up staying at the happy hour a little longer than most and didn't get to the game until midway through the second period. We were losing by two goals and wound up scoring two straight goals shortly after I arrived. Then, we won it in the third period. The next game on the following night, I didn't wear my costume because it was the first (of November). Halloween was over. We started losing and someone said, "We're behind because you don't have your costume on." I lived in the dorms, so I ran across the Quarter Mile and got my costume back on and returned to the game. So, you know what happens? We come back again to win, and, after that, it was almost like I was required to wear the costume.

He no longer was Steve Schultz, RIT student. He was the Grim Reaper, RIT hockey's good luck charm.

> After I graduated, I'm working full-time, and I figured, "Okay, I can go to RIT hockey games as a civilian again." Boy, did I get chewed out. So, I had to keep wearing it. Finally, when the first Gulf War arrived, I put it away, because I didn't feel right wearing a Grim Reaper costume at a time when soldiers are dying.

He did un-retire for one game—the final men's hockey game in Ritter Arena in February 2013.

> I managed to find my old RIT sickle, but I had to find a replica costume because the original one had been eaten by mice. It was a lot of fun, and the older alumni got a big kick out of it. Brought back a lot of fond memories.

After the RIT men's team won the Division II national championship in 1983, the separate corner crews agreed to merge. Schultz, the de facto leader of the southeast corner, met with Peter "Tucker" Lutz, the de facto leader of the southwest crew, at a springtime summit and decided there was strength in numbers.

"I guess you could say that's when it officially became known as the Corner Crew," Schultz said. "It made sense. Why have two competing cheer sections? Why not unite and create even more havoc? And that's what we did."

Over time, the Crew became more organized. The group staked out its spot to the right of the home team bench and put up a large banner with the warning: WE'RE LOUD AND OBNOXIOUS AT HOCKEY GAMES. That slogan found its way onto orange T-shirts featuring a variety of drawings through the years, including silhouettes of the Grim Reaper brandishing his sickle. New characters would emerge to carry on and add to the Crew's reputation. Among them was Alex Lewis, whose parents worked at RIT and took him to his first game as an eight-year-old in 1986. It was love at first sight for Lewis, and from that moment on, he knew he would attend RIT and become a regular at hockey games. One of the things that captured his fancy at his first game was a student named Mike, who led the Corner Crew in cheers and banged on a large wooden box with a broken hockey stick. "I thought that was so cool," Lewis said. "I wanted to be the guy who banged the stick, and eventually I did." Lewis, who graduated with a degree from RIT in hotel food management, eventually became known as "Stickboy." He would don an old, brown RIT jersey with "No. 5" on the back, and bang the wooden box whenever he felt the crowd needed a jolt.

Members of the Corner Crew show their school spirit.

Dave Faas also would become part of Corner Crew lore. He stumbled upon the RIT hockey team by accident during the 1989–90 season. "I was never a hockey fan, but that year RIT was making a run for the national title, and a friend said, 'Let's go see what all the fuss is about.'" It wasn't long before Faas was not only hooked, but doing his best to fire up the Crew. He wore a hockey uniform (No. 24), replete with a goalie's mask painted like a tiger. He earned the nickname "Big Goon" for his merciless baiting of opposing players and referees. Although Faas never attended RIT, he became the school's food service supervisor. "I just absolutely fell in love with the hockey experience there," he said. "It's been a fun thing to be a part of through the years."

Another Crew character who made a lasting impact was Chris "Headbanger" Millette.

"I don't know how—or why—he did it, but after every RIT goal he would pound his head against the Plexiglas," Schultz recalled. "Not the smartest thing in the world to do, but it definitely got people's attention and did get the fans fired up. Fortunately, that tradition was replaced with one where we rang a bell after each score. No danger of concussions with that activity."

After the corners merged in mid-1980s, the group initiated a number of new traditions. Besides erecting the "Loud and Obnoxious" banner and handing out T-shirts, they asked a keyboardist to play music during play stoppages. After the keyboardist graduated, Schultz bought a sound system, replete with speakers, and played Top 40 songs during breaks in the action.

The repertoire of cheers expanded, and continues to be altered till this day. Many of the early chants have fallen by the wayside, but some have stood the test of time, including the one in which a synthesizer makes a bus honking sound, prompting fans to jingle their keys and chant, "Start the bus!" For a while, the Crew published a magazine called *Shouts on Goal,* and featured articles by long-time members such as Laurie Barrows, Matt Gehrig, Mike James, Lerch and Schultz. Ads were sold and the money used to purchase an improved sound system. One of the more controversial issues featured a Lerch-authored story titled "Why I Hate Union." The back of the magazine featured a cut-out mask of Bruce Delventhal, who had guided RIT to the 1984–85 Division III national championship before bolting to take over as Union's head coach. "Bruce," recalled Lerch, "was not pleased." At the end of the '87–'88 season, the Corner Crew started the

Dave Faas, who wore a hockey jersey and goalie's mask to games, became known as the "Big Goon."

Fan's Choice Award, which was presented annually to the player who showed the most spirit and who really got the crowd going. Steve Mirabelle was the first recipient. The following year, the Crew expanded the award to include a women's hockey player as well. And in 1997, it

RIT

was renamed in memory of Dan Barrows, who had been a loyal supporter of the program for decades.

After renovations to Ritter Arena were made in the mid-1990s, the Crew moved from the southwest to the northwest corner. A new banner was created and the tradition of draping and rippling the American flag during the national anthem was started. Eventually, the school purchased a DJ system for Ritter, although Schultz still provided the music. As his start-up company, Pictometry International Corporation, began to take more and more of his time, Schultz no longer could serve as DJ, and others filled the role. In the mid-2000s, a small pep band formed and eventually replaced the DJ, providing music during pre-game, play stoppages and intermissions.

Over time, the Corner Crew decided to take its act on the road, with scores of Tiger fans carpooling to away games against hated rivals, such as Elmira and Oswego. Its most famous trip—and perhaps its finest hour—occurred at the Frozen Four inside Detroit's Ford Field in April 2010. Thousands of RIT hockey fans—many on school-chartered buses—made the trip to the Motor City, and assumed their usual positions in the corner of the massive football stadium that had been converted into an ice rink.

Although RIT was beaten decisively by Wisconsin in the semifinal, the Corner Crew kept cheering them on, entertaining the crowd of more than 30,000 with chants such as: "That's all right, that's okay, you're gonna work for us some day." Even after the Tigers were eliminated, the Crew and other RIT fans stayed for the other semifinal and the championship game. During the title game, they cheered just as loudly, sometimes for RIT, sometimes for one of the other teams. At one point, after Boston College had scored two quick goals in the title match against Wisconsin, Tigers fans chanted, "That's

Opposite: Whether disputing a referee's call or razzing an opposing player, RIT fans can be quite intimidating. Above: Waving a huge American flag during the playing of the National Anthem, and RIT's entertaining pep band are two enduring Corner Crew traditions.

how we felt," eliciting laughs from the crowd. Fans from several other schools were so entertained that they began joining the Crew in their cheers. "I remember fans from Notre Dame, in particular, coming over and trading their jerseys for our T-shirts and other Corner Crew paraphernalia," Schultz recalled. "If we had known we'd be in such demand, we would have brought a truckload of stuff with us and made a killing."

Members of the national media took notice, too. ESPN color commentator and former NHL player and coach Barry Melrose sang the praises of the Corner Crew during the national telecast and gladly accepted RIT's invitation to speak on campus the following fall. After each game, it's a hockey tradition to name three star players who stood out. One newspaper columnist was so taken by RIT's school spirit that he awarded one of his game stars to the Corner Crew.

The famed student cheering section continues to be hugely supportive of its beloved hockey teams. And its support extends beyond its chants. Through the years,

DAN BARROWS: HOCKEY AMBASSADOR

He didn't wear a mask or a costume to games. Nor did he pound a hockey stick against a box or bang his head against the Plexiglas to stir fans' emotions. Instead, Dan Barrows entertained RIT spectators and players and coaches with his countless hockey stories and words of encouragement. His endless supply of hockey tales and engaging personality made him as beloved a fan as RIT ever had.

"The sport had no greater friend, particularly at the high school level and at RIT," recalled longtime college hockey writer and radio analyst Chris Lerch. "I loved listening to his stories, and he had a million of them. I'd seek him out between periods and before and after games at Ritter Arena. And so did a lot of other people. The guy always had a smile on his face. The fans absolutely loved him, and so did the RIT players and coaches."

After Barrows died unexpectedly of a heart attack at age 62 on November 8, 2007, dozens of members of the Corner Crew attended his funeral. The Tigers held a moment of silence in his memory before their next game, and after they won their first Division I playoff game in overtime, linesman Chris Foote fished the puck out of the net, looked for Dan's widow, Laurie, in the crowd and flipped it to her.

Interestingly, Barrows had no interest in hockey until his father dragged him to a Rochester Americans minor-league game when he was a kid. "He went kicking and screaming," Laurie recalled. "But as soon as they dropped the puck, he was mesmerized." He was the reason she got hooked on RIT hockey and became the senior member of the Corner Crew. "My blood isn't red," she once said. "It's orange, in honor of RIT." Dan also loved high school hockey, and became the official historian and statistician for scholastic games in the Rochester area and throughout the state. He was posthumously inducted into the New York State High School Hockey Hall of Fame in Lake Placid, and the Corner Crew perpetuated his memory by renaming its annual fans' choice award after him in 2007.

School mascot RITchie conducting the Corner Crew.

the Crew has filled the role of booster club, too, helping raise money for Ritter renovations, the construction of the Polisseni Center and recruiting travel budgets. And Schultz, who kicked in a million dollars to jump-start the fundraising for the new arena and is a member of the RIT Board of Trustees, indicated he couldn't be more proud of what the Corner Crew has become.

> I'll never forget the scene after the team bus returned from Albany after clinching a berth in the Frozen Four. It was the middle of the night, but there were thousands of people out in the main circle on campus to greet the team. I had never seen anything like that at RIT. And it transported me back to my undergraduate days and all the fun we had rooting for the hockey team. It made me feel good to see that the school spirit and enthusiasm we helped get started was stronger than ever. It reminded me of how powerful sports can be in a positive way; how it can bring students and alumni together, and make you feel proud of your school.

WEST DIVISION III

8.

HOME SWEET HOME(S)

The brand new Gene Polisseni Center, christened just before the start of the 2014–15 season, is the fifth place the RIT hockey program has called home through the years. Interestingly, the school's first home rink—Blue Cross Arena at the War Memorial in downtown Rochester—continues to be a home away from home, serving as the site of the annual Brick City Homecoming Weekend Game, as well as the host rink for the Atlantic Hockey Association playoffs. In the late 1950s, when RIT launched its first men's club hockey team, the Tigers played the majority of their games on the road. Practice ice time was hard to come by because there were only a limited number of refrigerated rinks in the area, so the Tigers were forced to utilize the outdoor ice at Genesee Valley Park, often between midnight and 1 a.m. During the 1960–61 season, they did wind up playing a game at the park, against the University of Rochester, their crosstown rival.

Not long after officially being recognized by the school as a club team in 1958, RIT players Jack Trickey and Allan Shepard were able to convince the manager of the Ritter-Clark Memorial Building (now the Skating Institute of Rochester) to use the Spring Street facility for practice. The athletic center, which housed a rink and an adjoining gymnasium, had been built on RIT's original campus, in downtown Rochester, and opened with a figure skating exhibition in December 1955. The major benefactor for the project was F. Ritter Shumway. The building was named in honor of his grandfather, Frank Ritter—one of the original group of industrialists who established Mechanics Institute, the forerunner of RIT in 1885—and George Clark, a longtime director of Eastman Kodak Company.

Shumway had been a longtime figure skating competitor, who had won numerous medals in regional and national competitions. And the ice rink, though built to hockey specifications, was designed with figure skating as its main priority. The RIT hockey team was given permission to use the indoor rink for practices, with one stipulation: they couldn't use pucks for fear they would shatter the mirrors that had been placed around the ice so figure skaters could check their form. Trickey, Shepard and his teammates grudgingly agreed to the

Oppposite: Ritter Arena, on the Henrietta campus, served as RIT's hockey home for 46 years.

Ritter-Clark Arena, on the school's old downtown Rochester campus, was the original home of RIT hockey.

puck banishment, but managed to circumvent the rules by using balled-up rolls of tape as substitutes.

Around this time, the Tigers also managed to work out an agreement to rent out the War Memorial so they could play games on days when the building wasn't being used to host Rochester American minor-league hockey games or other events, such as circuses, religious conventions and National Basketball Association exhibitions and regular-season games. Ritter-Clark and the War Memorial continued to serve as the school's hockey homes until 1968 when the university reinvented itself, relocating from its cramped, one-block downtown campus to a sprawling expanse of land in the Rochester suburb of Henrietta.

The original Brick City architectural plans called for nine academic buildings and an athletic facility—initially called Shumway Arena after the man who donated a million dollars to help the new rink become a reality. But as he had done the first time he had dug deep into his pockets to help RIT build an ice rink, Shumway insisted the edifice be named after his grandfather, and before long the building was renamed Ritter Arena. The arena—which also included the attached Clark Gymnasium—was constructed without amenities in mind. In fact, it

HOME AWAY FROM HOME

The Rochester Community War Memorial, now called the Blue Cross Arena at the War Memorial, was the original site of RIT men's hockey home games, dating back to the program's origins in the late 1950s when the campus was located in downtown Rochester, just a few blocks away. In recent years, the arena has hosted the Tigers' annual Brick City Homecoming games, as well as the Atlantic Hockey Association's post-season tournament. From 2009 through 2014, RIT's Brick City game was one of the hottest sports tickets in town, drawing sellout crowds of 10,556 for each of those contests. The 2013 homecoming game against the University of Michigan set a record, selling out 15 days in advance of the opening face-off.

"At many colleges, a football game is the focal point of homecoming weekend," said RIT men's hockey coach Wayne Wilson. "But since we don't have a football team, hockey has come to fill that role. We like to use the opportunity to schedule the best programs we can—programs that certainly wouldn't have come to play us in Ritter Arena (capacity: 2,100) or maybe even in our new arena (the Gene Polisseni Center with a 4,300-person capacity). It gives us a chance to measure ourselves against the upper-echelon programs, and it gives people beyond campus, throughout the Rochester community, a chance to see us play in the biggest venue in the area. It's been a great, great atmosphere."

seemed almost Spartan with nothing more than a sheet of ice and bench seating wrapped in a horseshoe. Through the years, the building would be tweaked and made to feel less sterile, as Plexiglas replaced the protective wire netting and more spacious locker rooms were added, along with new coaches' offices, a training room, concession stands, a press box, renovated ceilings and improved lighting and sound systems. "It wasn't much at first, but it got the job done," said longtime RIT Athletic Director Lou Spiotti. "Over time, though, we added a lot of things that really gave it a homey feel. But, ultimately, what made the building were the people who occupied it—the great men's and women's hockey teams we had that played there, as well as our passionate fan base."

Ritter wound up housing the school's hockey programs for 46 years, with its final games being played in March 2014. And thanks to the quality of play—the Tigers hosted a combined five NCAA title games there—and the raucous Corner Crew and energetic pep band, it became one of the most distinctive arenas in all of college hockey.

"It made a lasting impression on me the first game I attended," said RIT President Bill Destler. "I could sense right from the start that it was a great college atmosphere. The enthusiasm of the students and alumni was contagious. You couldn't help but feel the school spirit."

Chris Tanev, who played on RIT's 2010 Frozen Four team and became the first player in school history to play in the National Hockey League, concurred with Destler. "It was bumping when I was here," Tanev told the *Democrat and Chronicle*. "We were a pretty good team and the fans were awesome. It was loud every night and it definitely got the guys going. It was one of the most fun places I've played in my life so far."

Ritter Arena was a barebones, Spartan building with few fan amenities during its first several years.

Those sentiments were shared by many of the members of school's vociferous cheering section. "I think it's the best atmosphere in (the Atlantic Hockey Association)," said Ed Trefgzer, the play-by-play man for men's hockey broadcasts on campus radio station WITR-FM. "People are so close to the ice, it's loud, it explodes, and it's been a great recruiting tool over the years, too. And, for the fans, it's just been a fun place to be."

Although hockey was Ritter's main event, with roughly 1,000 men's and women's games being played there through the decades, the building also hosted numerous other events, including rock concerts featuring the likes of U2, the Ramones, 10,000 Maniacs, Dave Mason, Cheap Trick and Elvis Costello. Comedian Jay Leno told jokes there, as did Bob Hope, during the university's 150th anniversary celebration. Olympic figure skating gold medalist Scott Hamilton staged an exhibition at Ritter, and commencement ceremonies and high school hockey championships also were held there.

College hockey, though, provided the most passionate memories. The men's team christened the building with a 7–4 victory against the College at Brockport on December 8, 1968. From that point on the Tigers experienced a true home-ice advantage, posting an all-time

Fans packed Ritter Arena (capacity: 2,100) like sardines. Over time, improved lighting and white paint on the walls helped brighten the building's interior.

PART-TIME JOE, FULL-TIME INSPIRATION

Joe Vicario loves posting inspirational quotes on his Facebook account. Among his favorites is one from late British Prime Minister Winston Churchill, who advised: "If you are going through hell, keep going." Vicario, a beloved student manager for the RIT hockey program, went through hell—and then some—but never allowed it to stop him. He's kept going forward, often smiling in the face of adversity. Vicario's hell has included Goldenhar Syndrome, which left him with a heart defect and without two organs, a thumb, and an ear. He has endured more than 30 surgeries, including ones in recent years for two different types of cancer. All of the vertebrae on his left side are fused with his neck, meaning he could never play contact sports. His left arm is shorter than his right.

Despite the daunting physical, emotional and financial obstacles he's been forced to overcome, Vicario has never bemoaned his fate. "I don't think negative," he said in an October 2013 interview with the *Democrat and Chronicle*. "My mom always taught me to be positive. I don't let anything get me down." The Buffalo native had hoped to follow in his father's footsteps and play hockey as his dad had with the Junior Sabres. But his condition prevented him from lacing on the skates. It didn't, however, stop Joe from becoming heavily involved in sports as a student manager at St. Mary's School for the Deaf in downtown Buffalo. He became so popular among his peers that he received 20 academic and athletic awards by the time he graduated in 2010.

He enrolled at RIT's National Technical Institute for the Deaf, where he majored in computer science. As a student manager for the men's and women's hockey teams, he does everything from hanging the uniforms to cleaning the locker rooms to carrying the coolers. His heavy course load, plus the three medical leaves of absences he's had to take, prompted men's coach Wayne Wilson to nickname him "Part-time Joe" because "the team never knows when he'll be around." Vicario loved the name so much he put it on his FaceBook page. "PTJ, that's me,'' he said with a smile. Wilson expressed his admiration for the manager.

Joe Vicario

> It never ceases to amaze me, not merely what he has overcome, but the way he has maintained such a positive attitude throughout. He has such tremendous perspective on things. I'll be having a bad day or one of the players will be struggling, and there's Joe giving us a pep talk, trying to lift our spirits. He truly is one of the most amazing people I've ever encountered.

record of 434–165–31 in the cozy confines of Ritter. Interestingly, the rink didn't provide an edge in some of the most momentous games played there. The RIT men's team lost NCAA Division III finals there in 1989 and 2001, and also lost in the 1984 semifinals in a four-overtime heartbreaker against Union College. The women also lost a national title game at Ritter in 2011, before avenging that defeat a year later when they won it all on home ice.

Randy Bloechl, a 1984 RIT graduate, was on hand for the majority of Ritter's highs and lows, spending 26 seasons doing play-by-play at radio station WITR-FM before turning over the microphone to his long-time partner, Trefgzer. "Hockey jumped on campus and people went crazy for it," he told the *Democrat and Chronicle* in a 2014 interview. "What I remember most are the guys I met through RIT hockey, guys I see 30 years later like Dave Burkholder, Gump Whiteside, Chris Johnstone. What's great about (Ritter) is everything is so close, you're right against the windows and you can see everything. The players love the fans and the fans love the kids right back."

It was difficult for Bloechl and many longtime RIT hockey followers to say goodbye to the Tigers' longtime home, but as the men's and women's programs gained national stature and made the move to Division I, it was apparent that a new arena would be needed.

FROZEN FRONTIER

In a way, it was like returning to their pond hockey roots. After all, in the late 1950s, when a small group of determined students were getting the sport off the ground at RIT, they were forced to practice outdoors at a rink at Genesee Valley Park, a few miles from the school's downtown campus. They even played a game there against their crosstown rivals, the University of Rochester.

So, when RIT officials agreed to participate in the 10-day Frozen Frontier hockey festival being hosted by the Rochester Red Wings minor-league baseball team at Frontier Field in mid-December 2013, they were actually repeating history—their own and the school's. Wayne Wilson, the longtime RIT men's hockey coach, felt it was appropriate for the athletes to join the festival.

> I would say the majority of the players who took part in those games at the Wings ballpark had played hockey on frozen ponds during their youth. That's why when they invited us it was a no-brainer. I'm glad we did it, and so are the players. It's an experience none of us will ever forget.

Opening face-off

"One of the big problems we had was the building was no longer big enough to accommodate the interest—not only on the RIT campus, but in the community at large," said RIT President Bill Destler. "Ritter's seating capacity was only 1,600, with standing room for about 500 more, and demand for tickets was exceeding that. We had a situation where people would have to show up hours before face-off in order to secure a good seat, and people from outside campus were reluctant to come because many of the games were sellouts. Plus, there was a need not only for added amenities, but also necessities. We needed more concession stands and more restrooms, and we just didn't have the space for those things in the

Ritter also hosted non-hockey events, including a rock concert by U2 and standup comedy by Bob Hope and Jay Leno.

RIT players line up for National Anthem

Goalie Mike Rotolo

The Frozen Frontier kicked off with a Friday night American Hockey League game involving the city's venerable minor-league team, the Rochester Americans. The next day, December 14, the women played a matinee game, losing 6–2 to Clarkson University, while the men played the nightcap, skating to a 2–2 tie with Niagara University. A crowd of 4,760 fans showed up for the men's game, which was played under frigid, snowy conditions that required numerous shoveling breaks to clear the ice.

"I was worried about rain, sun and warm temperatures (the week before when the mercury bumped past 60) and we got January," Wilson joked. "The conditions didn't exactly make for artistic hockey. We were literally trying to shovel the puck down the ice and into the goal."

Each team managed to do that twice. But the lack of artistry was worth the spectacle of playing hockey in the elements. "To be a part of this is pretty special," RIT goalie Mike Rotolo said afterward. "It really did remind a lot of the guys of their youth."

old place. And since we had elevated both the men's and women's programs to Division I, we needed to make a greater commitment through upgraded facilities."

Interest in RIT hockey reached an all-time high during the men's Frozen Four appearance in 2010, and that's when Destler and the board of trustees decided it was time to move forward with the idea of building a new rink. It was determined that an arena with 4,000 seats and standing-room-only space for about 300 more spectators would be ideal. Reserved chair-back seats would fill about three-quarters of the arena, and there would be six luxury suites, along with a full-service hospitality area and two large video boards on either end of the arena. The rink would be constructed just south of the student alumni union in the heart of the campus. Construction costs were estimated at $38 million, with $15 million being paid through revenues generated by hockey games and other events held in the multipurpose facility.

Steve Schultz, one of the modern Corner Crew founders and an RIT trustee, said he had long dreamed of building a new arena for the hockey program.

> Years ago, when I first started my company (Pictometry International Corp.), I said, "If this thing takes off and I make it big, I'm going to build us a new hockey barn." And when the time came, the trustees asked me if I was still game. I spoke with my wife and she miraculously said yes.

He and his wife, Vicki, who is also an RIT graduate, agreed to jump-start the fundraising campaign with a million-dollar donation.

That spurred other alumni to follow suit to lesser degrees, but the big boost came in November 2011 when RIT trustee Tom Golisano, in partnership with the Polisseni Foundation, gave $4.5 million to create the Gene Polisseni Center. Polisseni had been a prominent businessman, philanthropist and avid sports fan.

T-shirts were sold to help raise funds for the Gene Polisseni Center. RIT alumni Vicki and Steve Schultz jump-started the fundraising with a million-dollar donation. Hockey sticks, instead of shovels were used for the arena's groundbreaking, with RIT's Pep Band providing entertainment.

He had founded the Polisseni Foundation with his wife, Wanda, and had served as vice president of marketing at Golisano's company, Paychex, until his death in 2001. "I think this would have been one of his favorite gifts," his son, Gary Polisseni, said at the news conference announcing the donation. "This one would have truly touched his heart." Gene Polisseni had been a hockey fanatic his entire life. Family members said he started skating as a teenager, using magazines as shin pads. Gary spoke of his father's appreciation for the game.

> He built a makeshift rink in the back of his sister's house and started a league there. He just loved the sport. It's fast-paced and physical. That's what he enjoyed most.

Golisano, who spent eight years as owner of the National Hockey League's Buffalo Sabres, recalled afternoons at Paychex headquarters when his friend would suit up in Sabres gear in preparation for attending that evening's game in Buffalo. "Gene understood first-hand how sports could make a community feel about itself," Golisano said. "And I'm proud to help create a legacy dedicated to his passion for competition and camaraderie here at RIT."

A ground-breaking ceremony, which included dignitaries and members of the men's and women's hockey teams, was held on October 19, 2012 during Brick City homecoming. Less than two years later, on September 18, 2014, hundreds of fans attended a grand opening, amid the blaring trumpets of the RIT Pep Band and resounding

During the construction of the Gene Polisseni Center, President Bill Destler joined members of the men's and women's hockey teams in signing a beam that would be part of the building.

chants from the Corner Crew. "I am blown away," said Wanda Polisseni. "This is a dream come true for my husband because of his love of hockey and RIT."

Among the hundreds of attendees was Diana Tubman, a fifth-year psychology and marketing major and two-year member of the Corner Crew. She was especially pleased to see that one of the corners had been set aside for the student/alumni cheer group and that the rink had been outfitted with a new cast-iron bronze church bell that would be rung after each RIT goal. "Loving hockey is just a natural part of being at RIT," she told *University News* reporter Vienna McGrain. "And the best part about being in the Corner Crew is that you get to be extra loud." Perhaps no one was more excited that day than the RIT players. Marissa Maugeri, a forward from Ajax, Ontario, Canada, made her feelings known.

RIT President Bill Destler rides the Zamboni during the opening of the Gene Polisseni Center.

> It's crazy to finally be here after seeing it being built for so long. Now, we are even more excited to start playing our games here. We are thankful to play here and grateful for everyone involved who made this a reality.

Among those who helped the project come to fruition were benefactors Steve and Vicki Schultz. Steve expressed his appreciation for the new arena. "I think the thing I like most about the building is that it doubled the size of Ritter without losing the intimacy of the old place. You have more room to move around and it has the modern amenities you'd expect of a state-of-the-art arena, but you're still right on top of the action."

The RIT women's team played the first hockey game in the new building on September 29, 2014, losing 3–2 in an exhibition game to Pursuit of Excellence Hockey Academy from British Columbia. Tigers coach Scott McDonald called his team's effort "embarrassing," but he was feeling much better four days later when RIT officially christened the Polisseni Center with a 2–1 regular season-opening victory over Union College behind goals by Lindsay Grigg and Lindsay Stenason and 19 saves by goalie Ali Binnington. "Our effort and poise were much better tonight than on Monday," McDonald said after the game, which was witnessed by 1,021 spectators. The next night the men's team scored a 5–2 victory in an exhibition game against Brock University from St. Catharines, Ontario, in front of 2,973 fans as Garrett McMullen scored two quick goals and Jordan Ruby and Ken MacLean combined for 33 saves. Six days later, the men's team made it official, opening the regular season with a resounding 5–2 victory in front of 3,103 fans as Brad McGowan and Alexander Kuqali scored two goals

apiece and Josh Mitchell dished out three assists.

A new era in RIT hockey history was officially under way. President Bill Destler offered his predictions for the arena. "I think the Polisseni Center is going to have a dramatic impact on our programs. I think it will help us continue to attract outstanding student athletes. The building will enable more students and people from the community to attend games. I think it also will convince even better hockey teams to come in to play us because it's twice the size of Ritter. So, it's all good. I believe the new rink will enable us to strive for even greater accomplishments, and do so without compromising our high academic standards."

Destler had a chance to experience first-hand the impact of the Frozen Four on RIT. And that was followed a few years later by a Division III national championship

Wanda Polisseni is flanked by major benefactor Tom Golisano (beard, hands folded) and RIT President Bill Destler, at the opening ceremonies for the new arena named in memory of her late husband.

by the women's team. During the 2012–13 and 2013–14 seasons, Yale University and Union College won national Division I men's hockey titles. The fact that those academically demanding institutions were able to reach the summit of the hockey world, along with RIT's trip to the Frozen Four in 2010, and its monumental upset of top-ranked Minnesota State in 2015, has Destler dreaming big.

Asked if he thought the Tigers men's and women's programs could win national titles at college hockey's highest level, he said: "Not only do I think it's possible, I expect it. I definitely can see that happening."

A GREEN SEAT IN THE ORANGE HOUSE

Those who lived and played hockey with him at RIT from 1973–77 will tell you that Green B. Williams was a one-of-a-kind character—a young man with an engaging sense of humor and a zest for life. So it's only fitting that the former goaltender and honor student who was killed during a United States Air Force pilot training mission would be remembered with a one-of-a-kind seat at the Gene Polisseni Center. In Section 107, Row K, Seat 8 behind one of the goals, you'll find an orange-colored seat among the 4,000 blue-gray seats. The tribute to Williams was the brainchild of former RIT hockey teammate Tom Keene, who graduated in 1975. He got the idea from a seat honoring another Williams—famous baseball player Ted Williams, who was honored with a different-colored seat at Boston's Fenway Park to mark the 502-foot home run he hit there in 1946.

Keene broached the idea to RIT officials of raising $50,000 as part of the Tiger Power Play Fundraising Campaign for construction of the $38-million Polisseni Center, which opened in September 2014. School officials were all for it, and pamphlets with the catchy slogan "Let's put a Green seat in the orange house" were distributed. Thanks to the efforts of Williams' sister, Carla Williams Rossiter, as well as of family, friends, RIT alumni and fraternity brothers at Phi Sigma Kappa, the goal was met. Hockey teammate Jeff Begoon paid extra so that he and frat brother Jim Stanley could have their names inscribed on the armrests of seats 7 and 9 next to their late friend's seat. Begoon and Stanley were scheduled to be ushers in Williams' wedding in June 1984. The wedding never took place because Williams was killed in a mid-air collision during that training session on March 21, 1984, just eight days shy of his 28th birthday.

Green B. Williams

The goalie/honor student/good friend would not be forgotten. Starting in 2002, an annual award was given in Williams' name to the RIT hockey player with the highest grade point average. Now his legacy is further perpetuated by having a distinctive orange seat in the Polisseni Center that memorializes his commitment to his school, team and country.

APPENDIX: MEN'S RECORDS

YEAR-BY-YEAR

SEASON	WINS	LOSSES	TIES	COACH
1962–63	7	3	0	Jim Heffer
1963–64	17	0	1	Jim Heffer
1964–65	15	5	0	Jim Heffer
1965–66	14	4	0	Jim Heffer
1966–67	7	7	1	Jim Heffer
1967–68	10	8	0	Jim Heffer
1968–69	17	9	1	Daryl Sullivan
1969–70	9	17	0	Daryl Sullivan
1970–71	7	9	0	Daryl Sullivan
1971–72	11	9	0	Daryl Sullivan
1972–73	14	10	1	Daryl Sullivan
1973–74	11	13	0	Daryl Sullivan
1974–75	9	15	0	Daryl Sullivan
1975–76	12	13	0	Daryl Sullivan
1976–77	6	15	0	Daryl Sullivan
1977–78	8	8	1	Daryl Sullivan
1978–79	15	7	0	Daryl Sullivan
1979–80	12	10	0	Daryl Sullivan
1980–81	14	10	0	Brian Mason
1981–82	21	10	1	Brian Mason
1982–83	23	9	0	Brian Mason
1983–84	29	6	0	Brian Mason
1984–85	26	6	1	Bruce Delventhal
1985–86	31	6	0	Bruce Delventhal
1986–87	16	12	0	Bruce Delventhal
1987–88	14	15	1	Bruce Delventhal
1988–89	26	8	2	Buddy Powers
1989–90	19	8	2	Eric Hoffberg
1990–91	16	10	2	Eric Hoffberg
1991–92	12	15	2	Eric Hoffberg
1992–93	11	13	1	Eric Hoffberg
1993–94	20	8	2	Eric Hoffberg
1994–95	17	8	3	Eric Hoffberg
1995–96	25	6	1	Eric Hoffberg
1996–97	20	7	2	Eric Hoffberg
1997–98	19	4	5	Eric Hoffberg
1998–99	26	3	2	Eric Hoffberg
1999–00	21	7	1	Wayne Wilson
2000–01	27	1	1	Wayne Wilson
2001–02	23	2	2	Wayne Wilson
2002–03	19	4	2	Wayne Wilson
2003–04	13	7	5	Wayne Wilson
2004–05	13	10	1	Wayne Wilson
2005–06	9	24	2	Wayne Wilson
2006–07	21	11	2	Wayne Wilson
2007–08	19	12	6	Wayne Wilson
2008–09	23	13	2	Wayne Wilson
2009–10	28	12	1	Wayne Wilson
2010–11	19	11	8	Wayne Wilson
2011–12	20	13	6	Wayne Wilson
2012–13	15	18	5	Wayne Wilson
2013–14	12	20	5	Wayne Wilson
2014-15	20	15	5	Wayne Wilson
TOTALS	**891**	**501**	**86**	

Wayne Wilson

Eric Hoffberg

Daryl Sullivan

Andrew Favot

Dan Ringwald

COACHES RECORDS

NAME	W	L	T
Wayne Wilson	302	180	54
Eric Hoffberg	185	82	22
Daryl Sullivan	131	135	3
Brian Mason	87	35	1
Bruce Delventhal	87	39	2
Jim Heffer	70	27	2
Buddy Powers	26	8	2

CAREER SCORING LEADERS

DIVISION I

NAME	YEARS	GAMES	GOALS	ASSISTS	POINTS
Cameron Burt	2008–12	147	43	93	136
Simon Lambert	2005–08	104	55	77	132
Andrew Favot	2007–11	140	41	89	130
Dan Ringwald	2006–10	145	21	104	125
Matt Garbowsky	2011-15	128	48	66	114
Mike Colavecchia	2010–14	140	44	66	110
Brad McGowan	2011–15	150	46	64	110
Tyler Brenner	2008–11	108	55	47	102
Matt Smith	2005–08	104	53	46	99
Alan Mazur	2006–10	137	27	72	99
Greg Noyes	2010–14	150	24	68	92
Brennan Sarazin	2005–09	144	39	51	90

DIVISION III

NAME	YEARS	GAMES	GOALS	ASSISTS	POINTS
Chris Johnstone	1981–85	129	114	136	250
Peter Bournazakis	1997–01	116	100	129	229
Scott Brown	1985–89	130	103	122	225
Mike Bournazakis	1999–03	111	70	144	214
Pat Staerker	1996–00	121	76	134	210
Chris Maybury	1992–96	106	82	126	208
Dennis Lepley	1965–70	79	111	92	203
Ritchie Herbert	1983-87	102	88	114	202
Ken Vokac	1966–70	NA	94	102	196
Bobby Trowell	1981–85	122	96	90	186

Shane Madolora

Tyler Brenner

Mark Doughtery

Chris Johnstone

Steve Toll

Mike Bournazakis

INDIVIDUAL RECORDS

DIVISION I

MOST GOALS, SEASON: 27, Matt Smith (2007–08)

MOST ASSISTS, SEASON: 36, Josh Mitchell (2014–15)

MOST POINTS, SEASON: 54, Matt Garbowsky (2014-15)

MOST GAMES PLAYED, SEASON: 41, Brent Alexin (2009–2010); Dan Ringwald (2009–10); Chris Haltigin (2009–2010); Adam Hartley (2009–10); Chris Tanev (2009–10)

MOST GAME-WINNING GOALS, SEASON: 6, Tyler Brenner (2008–09)

MOST WINS, SEASON: 27, Jared DeMichiel (2009–10)

MOST SAVES, SEASON: 920, Jared DeMichiel (2009–10)

LOWEST GOALS AGAINST AVERAGE, SEASON: 1.93, Shane Madolora (2010–11) and (2011–12)

HIGHEST SAVE PERCENTAGE, SEASON: .935, Shane Madolora (2010–11)

MOST SHUTOUTS, SEASON: 7, Shane Madolora (2011–12)

MOST GOALS, CAREER: 55, Simon Lambert (2005–08) and Tyler Brenner (2008–11)

MOST ASSISTS, CAREER: 104, Dan Ringwald (2006–10)

MOST POINTS, CAREER: 136, Cameron Burt (2008–12)

MOST GAMES PLAYED, CAREER: 150, Adam Hartley (2009–13), Greg Noyes (2010–14), and Brad McGowan (2011–15)

MOST GAME-WINNING GOALS, CAREER: 13, Tyler Brenner (2008–11)

MOST SAVES, CAREER: 1,727, Shane Madolora (2009–12)

MOST WINS, CAREER: 41, Jared DeMichiel (2006–10)

GOALS AGAINST AVERAGE, CAREER: 1.99, Shane Madolora (2009–12)

MOST SHUTOUTS, CAREER: 13, Shane Madolora (2009–12)

DIVISION III

MOST GOALS, GAME: 6 Norm McEachern 1963–64 vs. Syracuse

MOST GOALS, SEASON: 39 Steve Toll (1996–97)

MOST GOALS, CAREER: 114 Chris Johnstone (1981–85)

MOST ASSISTS, GAME: 8 Maurice Montambault (1985–86) vs. Brockport

MOST ASSISTS, SEASON: 52 Mike Bournazakis (2000–01)

MOST ASSISTS, CAREER: 148 Mike Bournazakis (1999–03)

MOST POINTS, GAME: 9, Mike Bournazakis (2001–02) vs. Neumann; Maurice Montambault (1985–86) vs. Brockport

MOST POINTS, SEASON: 84 Steve Toll (1996–97)

MOST POINTS, CAREER: 250 Chris Johnstone (1981–85)

GAME SCORING STREAK: 29 Scott Brown (1985–86)

2008–09 RIT men's hockey team

1985–86 RIT men's hockey team

MOST HAT TRICKS, SEASON: 6 Steve Toll (1996–97)
MOST HAT TRICKS, CAREER: 9 Chris Maybury (1992–96)
MOST SHUTOUTS, SEASON: 7 Dave Burkholder (1983–84)
MOST SHUTOUTS, CAREER: 12 Tyler Euverman (1999–03)
& Dave Burkholder (1980–84)
MOST SAVES, GAME: 74 Marty Reasoner (1973–74) vs. Canton
MOST SAVES, SEASON: 1,091 Mark Dougherty (1969–70)
MOST SAVES, CAREER: 3,275 Jamie Morris (1996–99)
FASTEST GOAL: :03 Shawn Wilkins 2000–01 vs. Brockport
(from center ice face-off)

Tyler Euverman

TEAM RECORDS

DIVISION I

WON/LOST, SEASON: 28–12–1 (2009–10)
MOST WINS, SEASON: 28 (2009–10)
MOST CONSECUTIVE WINS: 12 (Feb.12, 2009–April 8, 2010)
MOST LOSSES, SEASONS: 24 (2005–06)
MOST CONSECUTIVE LOSSES: 6 (Jan. 28, 2006–Feb. 24, 2006)
MOST GOALS, GAME: 10 (Jan. 14, 2012) vs. Sacred Heart
MOST GOALS, SEASON: 148 (2008–09)
MOST GOALS ALLOWED, GAME: 10 (Dec. 10, 2005)
vs. Rensselaer Polytechnic Institute
MOST GOALS ALLOWED, SEASON: 132 (2005–06)

Dave Burkholder

DIVISION III

WON/LOST SEASON: 17–0–1 (1963–64)
MOST WINS, SEASON: 31 (1985–86)
MOST CONSECUTIVE WINS: 17 (1983–84)
MOST LOSSES, SEASON: 17 (1969–70)
MOST CONSECUTIVE LOSSES: 9 (1973–74)
MOST GOALS, GAME: 24 (Feb. 8, 2002) vs. Neumann
MOST GOALS, SEASON: 275 (1985–86)
MOST GOALS ALLOWED, GAME: 24 (1966–67) vs. SUNY Oswego
MOST GOALS ALLOWED, SEASON: 152 (1974–75)

APPENDIX: WOMEN'S RECORDS

YEAR-BY-YEAR

SEASON	WINS	LOSSES	TIES	COACH
1975–76	0	2	0	Dich Gordon
1976–77	0	10	1	Dich Gordon/ Skip Blicker
1977–78	1	8	0	Bob Green
1978–79	6	4	0	Bob Green
1979–80	4	7	0	Bob Green
1980–81	6	5	2	Tosh Farrell
1981–82	8	8	0	Tosh Farrell
1982–83	3	9	1	Bill Germond
1983–84	5	8	0	Glenn Collins
1984–85	8	2	0	Glenn Collins
1985–86	9	7	1	Glenn Collins
1986–87	8	9	1	Glenn Collins
1987–88	9	8	1	Glenn Collins
1988–89	9	7	2	Glenn Collins
1989–90	2	10	2	Jon Poulakis
1990–91	6	10	0	Julie Handzel
1991–92	6	9	1	Julie Handzel
1992–93	4	7	2	Julie Handzel
1993–94	4	12	0	Julie Handzel
1994–95	6	11	0	Julie Handzel
1995–96	13	4	1	Rick Filighera
1996–97	11	5	1	Rick Filighera
1997–98	11	6	3	Bob Filighera
1998–99	14	5	3	Rob Scuteri
1999–00	12	5	5	Rob Scuteri
2000–01	14	6	3	Rob Scuteri
2001–02	21	4	2	Rob Scuteri
2002–03	18	8	1	Rob Scuteri
2003–04	16	8	2	Mike Grainsky
2004–05	18	8	1	Mike Grainsky
2005–06	15	10	0	Mike Grainsky
2006–07	22	4	2	Scott McDonald
2007–08	19	7	0	Scott McDonald
2008–09	21	3	2	Scott McDonald
2009–10	19	5	3	Scott McDonald
2010–11	26	2	2	Scott McDonald
2011–12	28	1	1	Scott McDonald
2012–13	16	16	5	Scott McDonald
2013–14	20	15	3	Scott McDonald
2014-15	15	19	5	Scott McDonald
TOTALS	**453**	**294**	**59**	

Scott McDonald

Rob Scuteri

Glenn Collins

Julie Handzel

Tosh Farrell

COACHES RECORDS

NAME	W	L	T
Scott McDonald	186	72	23
Rob Scuteri	79	28	14
Mike Grainsky	49	26	3
Glenn Collins	48	40	5
Julie Handzel	26	49	3
Rick Filighera	24	9	2
Tosh Farrell	14	13	2
Bob Filighera	11	6	3
Bob Green	11	19	0
Bill Germond	3	9	1
Jon Poulakis	2	10	2
Dich Gordon	0	2	0
Gordon/Skip Blicker	0	10	1

ALL-TIME SCORING LEADERS

NAME	GOALS	ASSISTS	POINTS
Sarah Dagg	63	91	154
Alysia Park	79	74	153
Katie Stack	81	57	138
Kourtney Kunichika	54	82	136
Kasie Strong	53	83	136
Isabelle Richard	58	72	130
Jen Gorczynski	66	61	127
Kim Schlattman	41	72	113
Kendra Bredlau	48	64	112
Maegan Geypens	44	65	109

TEAM RECORDS

DIVISION I

BEST WON/LOST SEASON: 20–15–3, 2013–14

MOST WINS, SEASON: 20, 2013–14

MOST CONSECUTIVE WINS: 9
(Feb. 15, 2014 to October 10, 2014)

LONGEST UNBEATEN STREAK: 9
(Feb. 15 to October 10, 2014)

MOST LOSSES, SEASON: 19, 2014–15

MOST CONSECUTIVE LOSSES: 5 Nov. 20 to Dec. 9, 2012

MOST GOALS, GAME: 11 Jan. 18, 2013 vs. Sacred Heart

MOST SHOTS, GAME: 87 Jan. 18, 2013 vs. Sacred Heart

DIVISION III

BEST WON/LOST SEASON: 28–1–1 2011–12 (.950)

MOST WINS, SEASON: 28 2011–12 (28–1–1)

MOST CONSECUTIVE WINS: 17 2010–11
(Oct. 29 to Jan. 15)

LONGEST UNBEATEN STREAK: 23 2010–11
(21–0–2, Oct. 29 to Feb. 11)

MOST LOSSES, SEASON: 12 1993–94 (4–12–0)

MOST CONSECUTIVE LOSSES: 12 1975–77

MOST GOALS, GAME: 22 2/2/86 vs.
William Smith (22–1)

MOST GOALS, SEASON: 174 2001–02 (21–4–2)

FEWEST GOALS, SEASON: 12 1976–77 (0–10–1)

MOST GOALS PER GAME, SEASON: 7.4 1984–85
(74 in 10 games)

FEWEST GOALS PER GAME, SEASON:
1.09 1976–77 (0–10–1)

RIT women's hockey team 1987–88

Ali Binnington

Alysia Park

2011–12 captain Kim Schlattman, assistant captains Tenecia Hiller and Ariane Yokoyama

INDIVIDUAL RECORDS

MOST GOALS, GAME: 5 Kasie Strong, 1/19/02 vs. MIT; 5 Kim Eisenried 1/9/85 vs. Hamilton

MOST GOALS, SEASON: 32 Danielle Nagymarosi, 2006–07

MOST GOALS, CAREER: 81 Katie Stack, 2007–11

MOST ASSISTS, GAME: 6 Colleen Baude, 2/23/02 vs. MIT; Beth Perras, 2/2/86 vs. William Smith

MOST ASSISTS, SEASON: 42 Colleen Baude, 2001–02

MOST ASSISTS, CAREER: 91 Sarah Dagg, 2007–11

MOST POINTS, GAME: 8 Kasie Strong, 1/19/02 vs. MIT; Colleen Baude, 1/19/02 vs. MIT; Dodi Rabinovitz, 2/20/82 vs. Oswego

MOST POINTS, SEASON: 68 Colleen Baude, 2001–02 (26 goals, 42 assists)

MOST POINTS, CAREER: 154 Sarah Dagg, 2007–11

MOST SHUTOUTS, SEASON: 8 Elaine Vonderembse, 2001–02

MOST SHUTOUTS, CAREER: 19, Ali Binnington, 2011-15

MOST SAVES, GAME: 66 Laurie Davis, 12/10/82 vs. Clarkson

MOST SAVES, SEASON: 788 Ali Binnington, 2013–14

MOST SAVES, CAREER: 2,292 Ali Binnington, 2011-15

MOST WINS, SEASON: 19 Elaine Vonderembse, 2001–02

HIGHEST SAVE PERCENTAGE, SEASON: .959 Nicki Werner, 2006–07

MOST WINS, CAREER: 52 Elaine Vonderembse, 2000–04

LOWEST GOALS AGAINST AVERAGE, SEASON: 0.89 Nicki Werner, 2006–07

HIGHEST SAVE PERCENTAGE, CAREER: .941 Melissa Norris, 1997–2001

LOWEST GOALS AGAINST AVERAGE, CAREER: 1.11 Carley King, 2009–12

PHOTO CREDITS

Unless otherwise noted, photos are courtesy of RIT Archives or RIT Sports Information.

p. 13	Dylan Heuer
p. 27	Jean-Guy Noud
p. 32	Michael R. Soluri
p. 41	A. Sue Weisler / RIT
p. 57	Josh Barber
p. 70	Dylan Heuer
p. 72	Dylan Heuer
p. 74	A. Sue Weisler / RIT
p. 77 (top)	Mike Bradley
p. 77 (bottom)	Dylan Heuer
p. 78	Daniel Wodecki / *Reporter*
p. 79 (left)	Jeff Vinnick
p. 81 (left)	Mike Bradley
p. 81 (right)	Dylan Heuer
p. 83	Mike Bradley
p. 87	Dylan Heuer
p. 88	Mike Bradley
p. 89	Dylan Heuer
p. 90	Mike Bradley
p. 91	Mike Bradley
p. 92	Mike Bradley
p. 93	Mike Bradley
p. 94	Mike Bradley
p. 95	Mike Bradley
p. 97 (all)	Bryan Bennett
p. 98	Ken A. Huth
p. 100	Ken A. Huth
p. 103	Dylan Heuer
p. 104	Mike Bradley
p. 106	Dylan Heuer
p. 110	Ken A. Huth
p. 111	Mike Bradley
p. 113	Ken A. Huth
p. 115	Dylan Heuer
p. 116	Dylan Heuer
p. 120	Rich Banick / *Reporter*
p. 122	Dylan Heuer
p. 128	Dylan Heuer
p. 132	Dylan Heuer
p. 135	A. Sue Weisler / RIT
p. 136	Omar Phillips
p. 137 (top)	Dylan Heuer
p. 137 (bottom left)	Rugile Kaladyte
p. 137 (bottom right)	Max Hautaniemi
p. 138 (all)	A. Sue Weisler / RIT
p. 139 (all)	A. Sue Weisler / RIT
p. 140 (all)	A. Sue Weisler / RIT
p. 141	A. Sue Weisler / RIT
p. 142	A. Sue Weisler / RIT
p. 143 (bottom left)	A. Sue Weisler / RIT
p. 146 (top left)	A. Sue Weisler / RIT
p. 146 (bottom left)	Mike Bradley
p. 146 (bottom right)	Dylan Heuer
p. 148 (top left)	Mike Bradley
p. 148 (top center)	Mike Bradley
p. 148 (bottom left)	Lois Bernstein / *Reporter*
p. 156 (bottom right)	Ken A. Huth
p. 161	Charles Wainwright

SOURCES

NEWSPAPERS AND MAGAZINES

Rochester Democrat & Chronicle
Rochester Times-Union
University Magazine
The Reporter
USA Today
New York Times
Detroit News
The Hockey News

PERIODICALS

RIT men's and women's hockey guides, 1976–present
University News newspaper clip file

WEBSITES

ESPN.com
RITathletics.com
USAtoday.com
USCHO.com
NCAA.com
Wnyhockeyreport.com

INTERVIEWS THROUGH THE YEARS

John Absalom
Dan Barrows
Randy Bloechl
Dave Burkholder
Tim Butler
Bill Carey
Jared DeMichiel
Bruce Delventhal
Bill Destler
J. Roger Dykes
Dave Faas
Russ Firman
Chris Lerch
Chet Hallice
John Hawkins
Eric Hoffberg
B.J. Hull
Stephen Jaynes
Chris Johnstone
Blaise MacDonald
Brian Mason
Paula Hoffman McGinnis
Scott McDonald
Kristina Moss
Laura Oakley Beebe
Chris Palmer
Kristine Pierce
Buddy Powers
Marv Pozefsky
Marty Reasoner
Marty Reeners
John Reitzammer
Kim Schlattman
Steve Schultz
Allan Shepard
Al Simone
Lou Spiotti
Sheila Stevenson
Art Thomas
Jack Trickey
Bobby Trowell
Joe Venniro
Joe Vicario
Bill Whiteneck
Wayne Wilson

ABOUT THE AUTHOR

Scott Pitoniak is a best-selling author, nationally honored columnist, television correspondent and radio talk show host whose journalism career has spanned more than four decades. A native of Rome, New York and a magna cum laude graduate of Syracuse University, Pitoniak has written more than 20 books, including two previous works published by RIT Press—*Jewel of the Sports World: The Story of the Hickok Belt Award* and *Johnny Antonelli: A Baseball Memoir.* A member of four halls of fame and the recipient of more than 100 journalism awards, Pitoniak has been named one of America's top sports columnists three times by the Associated Press. He and his wife, Beth, reside in Rochester and have two grown children, Amy and Christopher, and one grandchild, Camryn Marie.

INDEX

Page numbers in italics indicate illustrations.

COLOPHON

DESIGN	Marnie Soom
TYPEFACES	Proxima Nova *by Mark Simonson* Palatino Linotype *by Hermann Zapf*
PRINTING AND BINDING	Thomson Shore Dexter, Michigan
PAPER	80# Huron Matte